Retiree Lifeline!

How to Get the Government Out of Your Pocket

Strategies Your Broker or Advisor May Be Missing

By Curt Whipple, CWS, CEP

First published by:

Financial Freedom Education Institute
Starting Point Publishing
41081 Ann Arbor Rd. E.
Plymouth, MI 48170
Phone: 734-844-3400

First Printing

ISBN 978-0-615-73294-7

Printed in the United States of America.

Additional copies may be available at special discounts for bulk purchase in the U.S. for church groups, corporations, Institutions, and other organizations. For more information. please contact: Financial Freedom Education Institute, 41081 Ann Arbor Rd. E. Plymouth, MI 48170. Phone: 734-844-3400

This book is printed on acid-free paper. It meets or exceeds the guidelines for permanence and durability of the Committee on Production Guidelines for Book Longevity of the Council on Library Resources.

Dedication

To my late father Marvin Whipple and to my mother Norah Whipple; Thanks for raising me as a person who cares and desires to serve others. Thanks too for raising me in a Godly home.

To my beautiful and loving wife Connie; I thank God he has given us each other to travel this journey through thick and thin. You're the best!

Table of Contents

Foreword

by Peter Nielsen, "Mr. Universe" and "Mr. America"

At the age of 15, I was diagnosed with Crohn's disease. I describe Crohn's disease as feeling like you have the stomach flu every day of your life. After a major surgery and many consultations with doctors, there seemed to be little or no hope for me. I was a very sick teenager. No one, including the doctors, seemed to know how to help me. At best, life looked very bleak!

But God had other plans! Very early in the morning, almost two very dark years later in January 1977, I angrily raised one fist to heaven while holding a razor in my other hand, and screamed a challenge at God to do something or I was going to take my own life. In the dark stillness of the moments that followed, I heard God say, "Give Me one more day, Peter, just one more day." That challenge began a life-long journey toward physical health, spiritual health and wholeness for me.

The journey led to winning over 50 body building awards, including Mr. Universe and Mr. America titles. I have also been known as the Health, Wholeness, and Fitness expert on nationally syndicated TV and Radio shows airing on major networks. Over the years, viewers have watched and heard my syndicated TV and radio show, "Peter's Principles," resulting in changed lives, because of our challenge to capture the principles of better health, and new hope.

On March 7, 2001 the Crohn's disease erupted to bring another challenge into my life. At 2:14 that morning my heart stopped beating for 43 seconds. During the miraculous recovery that followed God spoke clearly to my heart; "Peter, do you love and trust Me enough to boldly use your national platform to declare My Name, on your shows?" That was what I heard… Since then, I speak about the power of Jesus Christ to bring new hope for living in Health, Wholeness and Fitness, in the spirit, soul, and body.

The new TV ministry, "The Principles of Hope," which airs around the world now, began with that same challenge of eleven years ago. I enjoy telling anyone who will listen that hope is the confident expectation that God will keep His promises. I define hope as "having optimum positive emotions about those things in your life that seem to be impossible." Sometimes the change we face when we look at retirement can seem scary or impossible. Retirement is one of the biggest points of change in our life!

One reason people don't like change is because they get comfortable with where they are in life (in this case 30 to 40 years of a work routine). They get used to their friends, the money they make, their lifestyle, job or the place they live. And even if it's not perfect, they accept it simply because it's familiar. However, when we are not willing to plan for the future, the economy, our longevity, our retirement or mortality, we get stuck in life holding on to what God did in the past instead of growing and moving forward into what God wants to do in the future.

So be open to new things. Plan for your financial future. Always remember that just because God has blessed you where you are doesn't mean you can just sit back and settle there. He wants to do something new, in you and through you, but you need to have a game plan with an A-Team. He wants to see you grow, prosper and flourish. Embrace change and see the blessing that's in store for you!

To develop your A-Team you must recognize when God is trying to connect the dots for you. Sometimes that means getting out of your own way. When I met Curt Whipple a few years ago it was a blessing and I was quickly caught up in his passion to truly serve and help others. As we got to know each other more, I discovered he felt the same way about helping retiree's find "financial health" as I do to help as many as I can find "physical health."

You see, I believe that financial concerns in retirement can negatively impact your physical well-being. In the same way when people are struggling physically, it can negatively impact their financial well-being. Nobody dies of just old age, but if you live carelessly you will depart quicker. If you don't care about good health habits and exercise, or if you let financial problems worry you to death, then you only have yourself to blame.

Because of the many similarities that Curt and I share, I was excited to offer the foreword in this, his second book.

Retiree Lifeline can help anyone wishing to make sure that their financial future is more secure find the peace of mind for their retirement years. Whether you are approaching retirement or already have begun your retirement, the wisdom and strategies shared within these pages can truly help you create the retirement of your dreams. Curt shares in a very simple to understand language many financial advisors find difficult to do. He speaks in layman's terms. You will find his analogies and illustrations easy to follow and something you can put into practice right away.

I wish you the very best future possible both physically AND financially.

Curt has asked me to share my website with you as well. I would be thrilled to hear from you and to have some small part in helping you find success physically. Then Curt and I can both realize our dream and fulfill our passion of changing lives for the better.

Remember, it's not how we start that counts; it's how we finish. *Retiree Lifeline* can help make sure you finish strong. Don't let the fear of retirement stop you from enjoying the life God meant for you. In order to finish the race strong you need to cross your T's and dot your I's. You need to be mentally, physically, emotionally, spiritually, and YES... financially fit. You're reading this book for a reason. I'm sure that it will ignite a spark in you to have the passion you looked forward to retirement with. It is my hope you will live the purposeful life and retirement that you deserve.

The scripture tells us not to walk by sight, but to walk by faith.

" ...run in such a way as to get the prize"

(1 Corinthians 9:24, NIV)

www.petersprinciples.com

Retiree Lifeline

Inflation, Taxes and...

We are facing many problems in the United States as I write this book. I'm not sure these obstacles can, or will, be corrected.

The Federal Reserve has printed over three trillion dollars of new U.S. currency. This is a staggering number that has never been equaled in history. For many, hearing these numbers has become so common, that after a while we don't even know what it means. We hear millions, billions, and trillions, but do we really understand how much we are talking about or does it all kind of mesh together after a while?

First let's look at the numbers.

One million dollars looks like this: $1,000,000

One billion looks dollars like this: $1,000,000,000

One trillion dollars looks like this: $1,000,000,000,000

"Okay, Curt," you say, "that looks right. So what?"

Look at your wrist watch or a clock, and then ask yourself how long is a trillion seconds? The answer is 32,000 YEARS!!!

According to www.usgovernmentspending.com, over the last three years, our country has been running an annual deficit over around 1.3 Trillion dollars per year.

FY 2012:* $1,327 billion (est)

FY 2011: $1,300 billion

FY 2010: $1,293 billion

In addition, the scale of U.S. government money creation is staggering: according to an article published in the *Post-Autistic Economics Review* it amounted to $2 trillion dollars in 2009-10, with another $1 trillion in 2011. On September 13th of 2012 CNNmoney.com reported;

> The Federal Reserve announced plans to unleash more stimulus in its third attempt at a controversial program to rev up the U.S. economy. The policy, known as quantitative easing and often abbreviated as QE3, entails buying **$40 billion** in mortgage-backed securities ***each month***. The end date remains up in the air, as the Fed will re-evaluate the strength of the economy in coming months.

We just dealt with hitting a debt ceiling (a limit imposed by the government that would not allow more debt without a vote from congress) of 14.3 trillion.

Many of the voting public feels strongly that we need to cut spending or we may be putting our country on the verge of bankruptcy. Meanwhile, the government said it's not enough. So, they came to a deal on a new debt ceiling. In the 14 months that followed that vote to raise the limit, out national debt has since climbed to $16,149,960,401,546 (www.usdebtclock.org,10/5/12). The same source shows the *debt per family* in America now stands at **$700,608!** Many concerned Americans are looking for our leadership to cut spending not increase it!

A **deficit** means we are running in the hole the stated amount each and every year. **Debt** would represent the total accumulation of deficits. In addition, if you count our "unfunded obligations" (commitments we have made as a nation to entitlement programs like Medicare and Social Security) *USA Today* reveals the eye-popping numbers putting the overall figure of debt (including unfunded liabilities) at an astonishing $61.6 trillion. If 1 trillion seconds is about 32,000 years and we have $61.6 trillion in debt, I'll let you do the math for repayment.

I hope and pray for the sake of our country and our children's future that we can get proper leadership to finally put the country ahead of special interest groups and wasteful spending. I have never understood how basic household accounting says always spend less than what you earn, and yet some of our nations brightest people can't get it under control. I have my theories as to why, but I will keep that to myself for now.

Let's get back to the issue of printing money. What does it hurt for the Federal Reserve to print more money if they believe it will help the country? My answer is that they are affixing a bandage on an open wound.

There is only so much U.S. currency floating around the world at any one time and our dollar is given a value in comparison to other currencies based on the strength of our economy and other factors. If the Federal Reserve prints more money and adds it to the circulation of existing dollars, then each dollar is valued less. Printing more money impacts the current value of existing dollars.

Let me give you an example. If the U.S. doubles the amount of U.S. dollars floating around the world, the added dollars then makes each dollar worth less. If I had a one of a kind rare painting it can have a high worth. However if I discover there were two others just like it, the one I own is now worth less. The same holds true when the Federal Reserve prints more money. If they were to double the amount of American dollars in the world then the existing dollars lose value just like the painting. Each dollar is not as valuable as they once were. Let's assume the manufacturer of a pen or writing instrument has been selling pens for one dollar, and by doing so can profit 50 cents. Now assume the Federal Reserve prints enough new money to effectively double the amount of U.S. dollars circulating in the world. This makes each dollar now only worth 50 cents. The pen manufacturer must now raise their price to two dollars in order to make the same profit as before as each dollar they collect for the pen is now worth only 50 cents.

What is this called when everything goes up in price? INFLATION. I have read many articles touting both sides of the potential of coming inflation. On one side many claim due to the printing of money inflation is all but certain. The other side says that in order to have inflation we must have demand for goods and services in order to drive up prices. As of the writing of this book, the U.S. economy didn't create enough demand as many families and individuals are fighting just to make ends meet. I decided to look back in history for my answer and to formulate my own opinion.

From 1979 to 1980 when Jimmy Carter was President, we went through one of the worst inflation eras in U.S. history. According to www.inflationdata.com, inflation rose over those two years by a combined 24.8%. If it had stayed that high, the cost of things we buy would double every 5.8 years (using the rule of 72 which says divide 72 by the rate and the result is how long it takes to double). So what was the demand back then? Were we full of prosperity? No! By the end of 1982 the unemployment rate reached 10.4% (www.multpl.com)! In 2012, our current "reported" unemployment rate is about 8%. There were 25% more people unemployed back then and yet inflation still reached 10.4% (so much for the demand aspect). While demand can be a condition for inflation, in my opinion it is only one path to inflation. The other is the printing of money and the devaluing of the dollar which is what we are seeing today and seeing it in amounts never before seen in history. I personally believe and will put myself on the line to say, that somewhere between 2013 and 2017, we will see interest rates rise and inflation come into play. Later, I will discuss things you can be doing to prepare and hedge against this coming epidemic. By the way, I am not just talking about gold.

As you join me in reading the chapters that follow, I know you will find some answers you have been seeking in how to better manage your investments, finances and retirement dreams in light of these facts and the economy we find ourselves in.

I also hope and pray our government will learn to manage their spending and debt. That's one that I believe only prayer can resolve.

CHAPTER 2

What is it You Want?

Is retirement just around the corner for you, or are you are already there? Like most people, your goal is to have a successful and secure retirement. You want a retirement where you will never run out of income and can have the financial freedom to enjoy your life after work. Why, for many, does this seem so hard to achieve? Why does this create fear of the actual capability of achieving the retirement they have dreamed of? I will be addressing these and many more questions as we share time together. I will share with you what your financial advisor has failed to tell you that puts your retirement at risk. I will share a strategy that puts you back in control of your future.

It never ceases to amaze me how many new people come into our offices and are shocked by how much risk they are carrying in their investment portfolios. The number one reason for this is that your advisor has failed to communicate with you on a level you can understand. With the strategies in this book, you will once and for all learn how to communicate to your advisor what you do and don't want, and you'll forever be in control of how your money is invested.

If you will bear with me, I would like to start by going back to the beginning stages of designing the retirement you want. For many who deal mostly with a large broker/dealer, these critical steps are missed. Therefore, allow me to take you there. It really is the critical first step!

I once heard a person say that he could shoot the apple off another person's head better than the famed archer William Tell. That is provided you blindfolded William Tell, spun him around five times and pointed him in the wrong direction. You say "That's crazy! How can he hit a target he cannot see?" That's exactly my point! How can you achieve a retirement when you have no idea what you want or what it looks like?

What is it that you want? This can actually be looked at from two angles. What you do want and what don't you want. From all of my years in counseling retirees, here are the most popular responses for what we want: freedom to travel, visit relatives, have good health, and give back.

Freedom to Travel

Did you ever see the movie *The Bucket List*? It stars Jack Nicholson and Morgan Freeman. I found it to be very entertaining. Yet most important, it helps us see how we can sometimes be so busy in life that we never stop to dream and think about what it is we really want to do or accomplish before we pass away.

For many, retirement means the ability to travel. It's important for you to talk to your spouse or get with a friend and break out a pad of paper and begin to dream. Make your own "bucket list" of things you want to do and places you would like to go during your retirement years. Where are some of the places in the world or this country you have always wanted to visit but have never been? Within America, how about Niagara Falls? Go and hear the roar of the water. Take the cruise up to the base of the Falls. How about staying in a Bed and Breakfast in the New England states during autumn and enjoy the changing of the leaves to the reds, orange and yellow colors that can take your breath away. You could visit the Grand Canyon and ride the mules or if health allows ride the rapids of the Colorado River. You might want to see the Redwood Forest of California where the size and majesty of the trees cannot be explained. There are many other options like cruising the Smoky Mountains in a convertible, going to Disneyland, or Alaska.

When you think of the World, have you ever wanted to visit the British Isles and see the amazing green of Ireland or the streets of London? How about touring Europe to see the Eiffel Tower in Paris, the Swiss Alps, or the streets of Italy? You could visit the Far East or Australia? What would you do if you could? Dream… make your bucket list today! Don't put it off!

Ability to Visit Kids and Grandkids

For some this is easy as they live close. For others it is much harder. My wife and I have friends whose children live in China and other friends whose children live in Alaska. That could mean fewer visits. However, no matter where our children and grandchildren live, visiting them is typically a major goal or want. How often would you like to see your grandchildren? What would it take?

Have Good Health

Aging usually comes with our bodies breaking down over time. While it is inevitable that we will all someday die, we want to enjoy the best health possible along the way. Affording great health care is a key for most people in retirement. Paint a picture of what your health will be like over the first 10 years of retirement. Remember, you can't hit a target you can't see, even if it is in your mind!

Giving Back

For some the idea of giving back in a financial way or by giving of our time is critical. One of my clients for years volunteered for the American Red Cross. He got to see parts of the world he would otherwise never have seen. While it wasn't under the ideal circumstances, he spent many years serving others and touching lives. Do you have a charitable heart? Have you spent your life caring for your family, and are now looking to invest in the lives of others? I don't believe we should aspire to retire and do nothing. We should always long to retire to do something with the years we have left. The question is what is the something you plan to retire to?

Over the years, one common thing shared by all of my clients is that they constantly tell me how busy life is in retirement. It's not uncommon to hear them say, "I don't know how I ever had time for a job before. I seem to run from the time I get up until the time I go to bed." So you see, we all retire to something other than just lying around. Again, it's up to you to set the priorities of what you will be retiring to do. If left undetermined, vacant time never stays vacant. If you don't make the decision of how your time is filled, someone or something else will.

Again, from all my years of counseling, here are the most popular responses for what my clients do not want: to rely on children financially or physically, to run out of money, have an estate go through probate, or overpay on taxes.

Reliance on Our Kids Financially or Physically

No one wants to be dependent on financial help from their children. Therefore, proper planning and securing your retirement can make sure this never happens. While physically there is only so much we can do to remain independent, again the proper finances can mean never being a burden to our children.

To Run Out of Money

Financial security is one of the chief goals of every retiree. Not being able to pay our bills can be one of our main concerns. Not being able to afford a certain level of lifestyle can make for a long and frustrating 20 to 30 years in retirement. Later, I will share strategies that can help guarantee you will never run out of income for the rest of your life.

Have Estate go Through Probate

In some states probate is easier than others. However, in most cases it is far better to avoid probate if for no other reason than the privacy issues a trust can provide. There are many who think the best idea is to put your child's name on your bank and investment accounts or the title to your home. THIS CAN BE A VERY DANGEROUS MISTAKE! Later we will teach you the pros and cons of why, as well as the pros and cons of a Trust versus a Will.

To Overpay Our Taxes

There is never a time when reducing our taxes is more important than in our retirement years. The less we pay in taxes, the more income we have in retirement and the longer our invested assets will last. I am not saying we should not support our government financially. I am an advocate of only sharing with the government that which we legally owe. As long as we are following the law when we figure our taxes, and do so legally, it is only appropriate that our money last our lifetime.

For many, they believe reducing taxes in our highest earning years is critical. However, seldom do taxes destroy our livelihood while we are working. Yet in retirement, reportable taxable income can make the difference in an enjoyable retirement versus a retirement in which we struggle to make ends meet. Your Social Security Income could be tax free if you handle your income properly in retirement. Unfortunately it is a rare advisor indeed who counsels a client in this regard. Usually it is simply investment advice **not "income" advice**. I'm truly looking forward to discussing this later in some detail to help you achieve the highest possible income with the lowest possible tax.

Let me tell you a story about Bob and Ruth (I changed their names to protect their anonymity). When Bob and Ruth came to see me in 2004, Bob was a retired barber and Ruth was a homemaker. As you might guess barbers don't have a pension plan, so Bob and Ruth were living off of their combined Social Security which amounted to about $25,000 per year. In addition, they were utilizing some of their investments. The total amount of income they needed per year was $43,000 of which $25,000 was coming from Social Security and $18,000 from their investment portfolio. When Bob and Ruth first came to see me, I noticed that their investments were actually in pretty good shape. However, where they or their advisor had failed involved how they took their income and therefore paid their taxes. I suggested that we make a phone call together. We called one of their investment companies and I asked them to change one thing about their account. **We tweaked one thing and their taxes fell to zero.** They still had the same $43,000 in income, but they stopped paying any tax on the interest income and Social Security income. All because of one simple phone call. You see, it took a while but we had to help Bob and Ruth figure out what they needed and what they wanted. Once they realized they needed the entire $43,000 free of tax and got the proper advice, this was accomplished.

Have you ever heard the phrase "When a student is ready, the teacher will appear?" Bob and Ruth were ready. They couldn't make ends meet by paying taxes on their income. Bob and Ruth didn't care about stocks, bonds, mutual funds, or annuities. What they cared about was getting the income they needed and securing it for life. It's a great deal of fun to see them for their annual review each year. I ask them the same question. "How much did you pay in taxes last year?" Bob looks at me and gets a big old grin on his face and says... "Nothing!"

The first step is to determine at what age you would like to retire. The second step is to identify how much income you need in order to have the lifestyle you desire and determine what portfolio balance is required to provide that income. Keep in mind that you will need to adjust for inflation throughout your retirement years. Otherwise, you end up sliding toward poverty with each year you live.

Over the last 30 years, one of the most common things I have run into in the financial services business is when I start off by talking to someone and asking them a very profound question, at what age do they plan to retire. Mind you my clients are mostly over the age of 50 and those who are still working have a hard time coming up with an answer. The husband may look at his wife and say, "Gee, honey, I don't know. I've never really thought about it. What do you think?" The wife looks back at her husband and says, "You're the one who handles the money (or vice versa) what do you think?" The husband says, "I just pay the bills not plan our retirement." This can go on for quite some time before they both finally come up with an age they *think* they would like to retire. Then with a sheepish look on their faces, they look over at me and answer with a question rather than an exclamation point or period as they say, "65?"

The truth is most couples have seldom talked about it nor have single people thought about it. They each may have fantasized in their own minds when that day may be. However, they've spent more time planning their last vacation than they did talking about the day they plan to retire, which could easily be a 30-year plan or more not just a 7-day vacation.

Assuming you are already in retirement or have now come up with the age you plan to retire, as stated earlier, the next step would be to identify how much income you will need. For many couples, they have never even put together a household budget for today much less plan their income needs after they retire. You see there are so many things to think about surrounding ones retirement that they fail to understand the importance of professional help in planning this major event that in today's world could last 30 years or more.

This book is not being written with the objective of helping you identify your annual budget in retirement. A rule of thumb is that you will need approximately 80 percent of the income you had before you retire. Making a commitment one evening to sit down and put what you are spending on paper will pay off handsomely for your future. Make it a date. Go out for a nice dinner and then come home and start writing down your bills and payments. I think you will be surprised by how little time it will take. There are many good books on the market that delve into the subject of budgeting. I will leave each reader to their own to work out the details and the amount of income you will need for your retirement. The key is to at least identify some amount of income it would take to give you the retirement lifestyle you seek.

Once you identify the income needed, you must now focus on what amount of money you must have in your investment portfolio in order to draw the income you desire or need. Once that is determined, you then must factor in inflation. You cannot simply say, "I need $50,000 per year in addition to Social Security to have the income I need. With 5 percent interest calculated, I'll need one million dollars." If you retired this way, you would slowly be slipping into poverty. You must plan for inflation and also look for inflation hedges for the years that inflation accelerates beyond its average of 3 to 4 percent over time. If this last paragraph leaves you confused, I don't blame you. However, hang in there as later when we get to investment strategies, I will be discussing some investment vehicles that will help you when these times appear.

I once had a single lady who came in for her first visit with me. She was living on $30,000 per year and had over one million in her investment portfolio. When I asked her why she was struggling on so little income while having a sizable investment portfolio with which to support her needs, her answer was the same as many who have since followed her. She said, "I am afraid I may someday run out of money and therefore want to use as little as possible, just in case."

I am concerned by how many people have the "cross my fingers" approach to their retirement. They have no idea what they can and can't afford to do in retirement. Some live like paupers on as little as possible for fear they will run out. Others live above their means and are on a one-way ticket to financial disaster and don't know it.

In this book, I will teach you how to manage your money so that you will always be in charge of your financial life. I will teach you how to, in as little as 30 minutes **each year**, *know exactly* where you stand. You will know how much you can afford to spend each year. You will know if you are ahead of the curve, right on track or behind.

I will teach you investment strategies that will help you get what you want, avoid what you don't want and never be totally at the mercy of a financial advisor for proper decision making again. Please don't misunderstand me. I believe to do things right, a qualified advisor can be critical and well worth their time and fee. However, too many retirees put their entire faith in the advisor (be it a CPA, CFP, CWS, or any other financial advisor) and really don't have any idea if the advisor is doing what they have asked them to do or if the advisor is doing what he or she wants or thinks is right. A professional advisor is not there to do what they think is right or wrong. They are in your life to educate you, give you the pros and cons of your options, and guide you in achieving YOUR goals not theirs. A professional financial advisor is like an architect who is there to help you design your retirement according to your specifications.

You must have a plan in retirement. Without one, you are "unemployed!" Let's look at it another way. If you were 45 and suddenly lost your job, how would you react? Would there be panic? I imagine one of the first things to cross your mind would be how will I pay my bills? How will we make the mortgage payment? What about our cars? Losing one's job can be one of the most financially traumatic events we can face.

Not having a planned and structured retirement is really the same thing. Without a retirement plan, how will you pay your mortgage? How will you buy your groceries? The questions can be the same. Yet for some reason, most of us don't even stop to think about the retirement issue seriously enough until it's too late to do anything to correct it.

This book is not being written with the idea of teaching younger adults how to build their retirement. It is being written with two objectives in mind.

First, if you are behind financially on planning for your retirement, is there anything you can do to catch up? Let's say you are 55 and want to retire at 65. To get the income desired, how much do you need to have in your investment portfolio? I will help you identify those issues. In addition, I will be offering ideas of things you might consider doing to help you redefine your retirement and help catch up to where you should be as you strive to achieve your dreams.

WHAT IS IT YOU WANT?

What is the Second Objective?

Please know the problem may not be yours alone. If you have many questions left unanswered, you must begin to ask if you have the right financial advisor and if your advisor has been asking the right questions. Later in a different chapter I will share with you how to find the right advisor. Our first meeting with a new prospect is a meeting that goes both ways. The prospect is trying to decide if we're the right advisor for them, and we are trying to decide if we are the right advisors for them and can truly help them. The way we can help this person is to ask a lot of questions.

Do you know what you want? In the next chapter I will be taking you through a question and answer session just as if you were sitting in my office. If you have taken the time already to identify some or all of the things you want, great! The next chapter will help us expand upon those answers.

CHAPTER 3

Signs that Your Retirement Plan is in Danger

Remember the year 2008? If not, you didn't have any money invested anywhere. The stock market fell 37% that year. Many people I met with coming from other financial institutions had lost as much as 50-60% of their portfolio in a single year.

Regardless of how much money you may have lost in 2008, there are eight indicators that you can focus on that would help you identify if you were taking too much risk in your portfolio and if your retirement plan was in danger.

Indicator 1:

You either looked at your accounts every day OR you wouldn't look at them at all.

Many could not believe that this was happening to them. If you looked at your account every day then you could be considered a sadistic person who loved pain. However, you couldn't help yourself. Your broker would constantly say one of two things: a) Just hang in there, it's going to come back, or b) You never invest for the short term in the market. Then they would go on into his or her memorized speech about how over any 20 year period of time the market is the best place to be.

If you were 25 years old, this **may** have been good advice. However, for someone within 10 years of retirement or God forbid already retired, this is a disastrous statement by any financial advisor.

This "advice" from brokers led many to stop looking at their accounts. When their monthly statements came in, they would either take a deep breath and peek, only to find that pit in their stomach again or they would refuse to open the statement and just pile them up in the corner. Their broker, was telling them to hold on. **This is a sign your retirement plan is in danger!**

Indicator 2:

You lost more than 15 to 20% of your investments value in 2008.

Later in Chapter 6, we will be talking about strategies to better protect your portfolio from a major market fall. We'll be discussing how you can be back in charge of just how risky your investments are instead of solely depending on your broker or financial planner. Don't get me wrong, this is not a book designed to beat up on financial professionals, after all I am one and most people can benefit from their input and advice. However, you should never put ALL of your faith in your advisor leaving your future totally in their hands without you having some say. Chapter 5 will help you learn how to take charge of your portfolio and manage the risk according to your risk tolerance, not the risk tolerance that a planner thinks is the right one for you.

When clients come into our office, I will many times ask them a simple question, "On a scale of 1 to 10, with 10 being your willingness to take risk on your investments and 1 being you hate risk of any kind, what number would you be?" Invariably, I would get a higher number. However, after asking some additional questions I would identify that the number was actually much lower than they first suggested. The only way to properly identify their true risk tolerance was with more in depth questions.

The next problem is that the gap between what your advisor sees as the appropriate investments for your risk tolerance level and what you would see as the appropriate investments. This gap can often times be worlds apart.

I have on countless occasions had prospective clients come for their initial interview and identified them as a three on a risk level of 1 to 10 only to find that the financial advisor had them invested at a level of 7. Time after time, potentially new clients would come in having lost 30-50% of their portfolio only to have them tell me, "I told my advisor I didn't want that much risk." In fairness, sometimes they were right about that statement. Other times, they only became that conservative after losing so much money. Either way, I believe it is important to teach consumers how to monitor the level of risk they are in and what a properly diversified portfolio matching their risk levels looks like. It's time for all investors to be taught how they can once again be in control of these issues instead of solely depending on their financial advisor to pick what the right investments and level of risk is for them. After all, it is not the advisors money. It's your money, and they will almost always be willing to take more risk on your money than you may want to. **Losing 15-20% or more in your portfolio in 2008 is a sign your retirement plan is in danger.**

Indicator 3:

Your broker or financial advisor tells you to "just hang in there."

If you ever hear this advice from your broker or advisor, then you could be taking too much risk. This is not to say that a well-designed financial plan won't ever lose money. If that's the case, it's not a well-designed plan. Any properly designed "financial plan" will most likely have some elements that will lose value at some point. However, the key is how has your overall portfolio performed? If you have twenty different investments in your portfolio and investments number 2, 5 and 12 lose some value, but the other 17 areas increase in value thereby meaning your portfolio either broke even or gained, you have a well-designed portfolio.

I many times must admit, that my more conservative investors will call if a similar occurrence like the one just stated happens. They don't like the fact that the three accounts mentioned above lost ANY value. I respond by telling them why this happened and what the outlook for the future is on those three accounts. If I believe they will do well in the future, I will communicate and educate them as to why they should hold onto those investments. Once I do this, they then can make an educated decision as to what they wish to do at that time. **But, it's their decision not mine.**

Other times, I will recommend they eliminate a position or make a change. But in all cases, patience and proper education are key. However, in no case do I say, "just hang in there." That is the advice you get from one of two advisors: a) the one who is lazy and thinks of themselves as so much smarter than you so you should just trust them, or b) the one who has no idea why the investment did what it did and has no good advice on what to do out of ignorance. **Either way, if you ever hear the words "JUST HANG IN THERE," it's a sign your retirement portfolio is in danger (and you may want to consider a change).**

Indicator 4:

Your broker or financial advisor fails to call you on a basis set by you.

One of the most common complaints I hear from potential clients is that they never hear from their financial advisor or broker. You should be getting a call each and every quarter from your advisor to review and discuss your account. The only time this should not be the case is if you, the client, wish to be contacted less frequently. The investment world is far too volatile in today's economy to live by the old "buy and hold" and call me once a year approach. I have some clients ask me to only call or visit with them semi-annually, even a few that say once per year (although these are the clients who carry virtually no risk in what they have chosen to do). However, unless told differently, quarterly calls are the standard. Markets move every day and to review your investments less than quarterly is a dangerous path to be on.

Does your broker call you more than quarterly? You would think this is wonderful to get that kind of service from them. However, this could be a sign of a dangerous amount of risk. Moving money on more than a quarterly basis would indicate that in order to succeed, it requires constant supervision. More importantly it could be commission motivated and not in your best interest.

Therefore, calls from your advisor too often could mean more risk. If they call you less, it would be because you requested it or the advisor is too busy finding new clients or just doesn't care enough and is a sign your retirement plan could be in danger.

Indicator 5:

Your portfolio is tied mostly to Wall Street or "stocks, bonds and mutual funds."

In Chapter 5 we will again look at this in more detail. However, check your statements and ask yourself if each investment you have represents only a stock, a bond, or a stock or bond mutual fund. **If the answer is yes, then you are taking a potentially dangerous amount of risk in your portfolio. See Chapter 5 for more details.**

Indicator 6:

You depend on your bond portfolio to protect you in hard times.

From 1981 to 1999, for a period of almost 20 years, the public was taught that bonds are the place to be when times get tough. Most of the public when asked would say that their advisor had told them that he will "watch" their money for them and when times are good increase stock holdings. Then when times get bad he would decrease the amount of stocks in the account and increase bond holdings for greater safety. There are three problems with this:

- This isn't 1981 through 1999. Times have changed.
- They never truly "watch" your money.
- You end up hearing "just hang in there" which wouldn't be the case if they truly were watching your money.

Why did it work over the past 30 years? Because bonds have an inverse relationship to interest rates, ask yourself this question, *when during your entire lifetime have interest rates ever been lower than they are today?* Answer: NEVER! For the past 30 years, interest rates have for the most part been falling. This means that bonds have done well and did actually provide a safe haven for money as the stock market became too risky. However, with rates at their lowest point in any living generations lifetime, what are the odds of rates continuing to go down versus going up over the next 3 to 5 years? The answer by every audience around the country I have spoken to is "there is an excellent chance interest rates will be going up not down". Since bonds do the opposite of interest rates, then this would mean very bad news for the future of bond values (especially bond mutual funds) in the years to come.

So, now where will your advisor move your assets (if they even do) to protect them from a falling market? Most advisors have no idea and still show no concern over learning about alternative strategies and investments to better protect you.

If your advisor is still suggesting that you use bonds within your portfolio as THE alternative to a falling market, this is a sign your retirement plan may be in danger.

Indicator 7:

You worry a lot about money.

Do you find yourself often thinking about your money or feeling fear about your ability to retire? If so, this could be a sign that your retirement plan is in danger. It also would stem from three possibilities.

- Your fear is due to being invested in more risky positions than you would like.
- You really don't understand what you even are invested in.
- You don't have a clear cut plan to achieve your financial objectives.

1. Your fear is due to being invested in more risky positions than you would like

We have already covered this earlier in this chapter. It's time for a change of advisors who will be able to give you more comfort in your portfolio allocations

2. You really don't understand what you are invested in.

If this is the case, your advisor is not educating you nor calling you as often as they should. This should lead you to question, "Why am I paying them?"

3. You don't have a clear cut plan to achieve your financial objectives.

This results when your advisor never presents a well-drawn up "plan" on how to help your reach your objectives. Instead, they are *selling* investments not presenting strategies and plans. There are no goals or targets determined. There are no hard targets along the way or dates to achieve certain objectives. There are no indications of points that must be reached along the way to help you know if you are on track to reach your ultimate goals instead of waiting to the end only to find out you have fallen short of your retirement goals. Now it is too late! Your approach designed by your planner is "Trust me to do what's right" and your left with nothing more than hoping you can reach your dreams. It's time to uncross your fingers and find another advisor.

If you are worrying often about money or your ability to be able to retire, your retirement plan is in danger.

Indicator 8:

You find you are short with people more than usual.

Do you find yourself short with others, on edge, more critical than usual? Family members are asking, "What's up with him or her?" This could stem from many reasons, not just your investments.

However, if most of life seems normal with the exception of your concern over retirement needs or money, then this could be a sign your retirement plan is in danger. Maybe it's time for a change.

CHAPTER 4

Why Most Retirement Plans Will Fail and How to Make Sure Yours Isn't One of Them

Most advisors who are advising today have only been in the business since 1979 or thereafter and therein is the problem! While we all believe in experience as a critical factor in getting good advice, in the financial services world it can hurt you if your advisor hasn't continued to grow in their knowledge during those years. Let me explain.

Most of you reading this book will remember the inflationary times we came through during Jimmy Carter's era as President of the United States. As mentioned before, 1979 to 1981 were some of the worst periods of inflation in our nation's history. Inflation reached the level of 21.5% at its peak. At that rate, the cost of goods and services were doubling every 3.5 years. While peak inflation didn't last long enough to cause that to come true, we can't forget the days when banks were paying 16% interest on a certificate of deposit.

You probably are thinking if I could only get 16% on a bank CD today, I would dump the stock market and put all of my money into CD's. If you did, you would be losing money at the rate of 5% per year with inflation over 21%. So, it's not quite as good as you first may have thought when you look at it from that standpoint.

What does this have to do with the potential failure of many retirement plans? In Chapter 3 I talked about the relationship of interest rates to the value of bonds. Let's look a little closer at how most advisors have represented their clients over the last 30 years.

You may recall a visit like this one. You went in to see your advisor and they drew a pie chart like this.

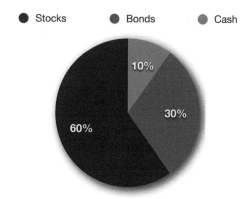

They said, "When the market is going well, we will increase your stock holdings and decrease your bonds and cash. However, if the market looks scary, I will call you and let you know that we need to reduce your stock holdings and increase your bonds and cash. This way we can make sure that you are always riding the positive swings in the market by overweighting stocks in the good times while overweighting bonds in the bad times to protect you when the market goes down."

Let me ask, how did that worked for you in 2008 when the market fell by 37%?

Most people have heard the famous line that all stock brokers are taught to say when they don't have an answer to you losing your money. We have referred earlier to the famous line, **"Just hang in there. The market will come back!"**

Isn't it easy to say that when it's not YOUR MONEY that's losing 37% of its value? What happened to the idea that your bonds would protect you? Why didn't your advisor call and recommend more bonds? Most likely they were too busy with their next prospect.

If they aren't moving your money as they promised, then they have you in a "Buy and Hold" Strategy. Why? Because they tell you what to buy and then you are supposed to just hold on to those investments forever. If that's the case, what good is it to have a financial advisor? When do you ever need a professional's advice again if all you are to do is sit on what you are first sold?

To me the greatest injustice is how brokers and financial planners seem to give the same advice to all age groups. They find stocks, bonds or mutual funds that they truly like and then sell those investments to all of their clients regardless of age or financial goals.

Is the buy and hold strategy the right strategy for every investor and under all financial circumstances? Or, is it simply the only advice brokers have known for the last 30 years? Unfortunately, I believe it is the latter.

Why then do so many brokers teach a buy and hold strategy for your retirement? I believe it's a) what they were taught to teach, or b) all they have known to do during their careers.

If that's all they know, how can they be expected to teach you anything different?

I must admit, that the buy and hold strategy worked well in the 80s and 90s. The reason for this is that we had the greatest period of prosperity and economic growth we have ever known as a nation. However, I don't believe it will work for at least another 6 years and maybe not for another 15 years.

Therefore if you are in or nearing retirement understanding, what I am sharing in this chapter could make or break your retirement years. It can be the difference between a great retirement and ending up depending on your children or falling into poverty. The buy and hold strategy hasn't worked as a strategy for the past 11 years. Here is why.

Bonds have an inverse relationship to interest rates. When interest rates fall (as they did from 1979 to 2012), bonds went up in value. Therefore, when a broker showed you the pie chart with stocks, bonds, and cash, it was a good strategy. If stocks happened to fall while interest rates were falling, your bonds would increase in value and protect some of the losses you realized in your stocks. Also, we were in a 20 year bull market from 1981 to 1999. While some might argue the idea of a 20 year bull market, with little exception the stock market went from 1,000 to over 11,000 during that period of time. That's a 1,000% return and one of the greatest bull markets we may ever see.

However, sometimes the longer the number of years the market climbs straight up, the longer the down swing that can follow. You may have heard it referred to as a bubble. That bubble began to burst in 2000 when the stock market fell over 9%. In 2001, it fell another 11%, and in 2002 it fell another 22%. Total the losses up without compounding them and that equates to over a 42% loss. Then in 2008, the market fell 37% in one year. However, what many people missed was that it fell another 22% in the first ten weeks of 2009 for a total uncompounded loss of almost 50%. For retirees, this was financial suicide. What did their brokers say? "Just hang in there!" Hanging in there makes sense for those who have 10 years or more until they retire. For those in retirement or close to it, it can destroy them.

I believe for at least the next 5 and possibly 16 more years we will continue to see the same type of market that we did from 2000 to 2011. I base this on two major premises.

- I believe the current state of our economy currently offers no hope in the near future of a possible bull market. Consider that in the first three months after Congress raised the debt ceiling that they have spent 700 billion more than they earned which puts us on pace for an annual deficit of 2.8 trillion dollars for one year. Our total debt in 2012 exceeds 15 trillion dollars. We are witnessing economic instability in Europe with Greece on the verge of collapse and closely followed by Italy, Portugal, Spain, and Ireland. The dollar is struggling against other currencies and there is talk of no longer using the dollar as international currency. Does this sound like the beginning of a bull market?

- We have been in four sideways markets in history (I will teach you more on a sideways market later in this chapter). The shortest one was 16 years and the longest one was 27 years. We are now in the 11th year of this current sideways market which could mean 5 to 16 more to go.

If your advisor doesn't see this or understand the change and continues to advise you in the same way he or she has over the last 11 years, it could destroy your retirement! Here's why. As I stated earlier, Interest rates are now at a level so low, no one reading this book has ever witnessed in their lifetime. Bank savings accounts are paying one quarter of one percent. CD's are paying less than 1% interest in most cases. Mortgage rates are in the 3% to 4% range.

When I got my first mortgage as a newlywed back in 1979, my mortgage rate was 12%. I believe we are about to see these rates again and a period of inflation as we have never witnessed before.

One reason to expect inflation is the printing of money by the Federal Reserve. For a period of 48 years, from 1960 through 2008, the U.S. printed on average 6.6% new money each year. For each

$100 of U.S. currency floating in the world, they would print $6.60 of new money while taking some out of circulation as old and worn out. In just the first seven months of 2009, the government printed 109% of the U.S. money.

That means for every $100 of U.S. currency floating in the world on December 31, 2008, by July 31, 2009, they printed $109 of additional money. What does this mean?

I believe it is worth repeating that as a result of doubling the amount of U.S. money in the world, each dollar is now only worth .50 cents. To put that into perspective, imagine an ink pen in your home that possibly cost you $1. In order for the manufacturer to provide the same pen to you that you bought for $1, he must now charge $2 to get the same $1 as before. Why? Each dollar is now only worth 50 cents due to the fact that there is now double the U.S. currency in circulation.

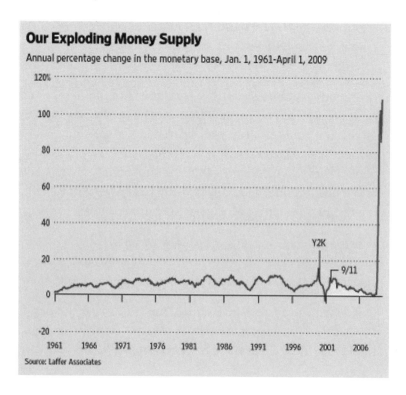

Our Exploding Money Supply

Annual percentage change in the monetary base, Jan. 1, 1961-April 1, 2009

Source: Laffer Associates

Now, what do you think that would do to a retiree trying to make ends meet on a limited supply of assets if their income was cut in half by inflation?

Let's get back to the buy and hold strategy. Imagine now that your stock investments are falling (which they will again) and interest rates are climbing. What does that mean for your bond portfolio that your advisor believes in so strongly? If your bond holdings are in specific bonds with maturity dates, it means bad news if you were to ever need to sell them as they will all be losing value right along with the stock market. If your bonds holdings are all in mutual funds, it means extremely bad news as there is no set date of maturity in which you get your principal back. They have so many bond holdings within a mutual fund that the share price is adjusted as people sell out of the funds and there is no opportunity to hold each bond in the fund until they mature.

Please don't misunderstand me. Bonds are great investments when held at the right time for the right reasons and in the right economic environment. I don't think long term bonds or bond mutual funds would be the right investment for many people with the threat of rising interest rates and inflation.

You might be thinking, "Well why not hold just short term bonds and then I don't have to worry about losing money due to rising interest rates." Your assumption would be correct, however, now all you have to do is worry about earning a mere 1 to 2% (due to the bonds being a very short duration) while inflation is taking off. That still means you're in a losing position.

What does this mean to the retiree? If your broker is giving you the same advice he was giving you 10 and 20 years ago, you need a new broker who is current and investing his own time and money into strategies that will help you weather the economic storm we find ourselves in.

Which way will the market go and what does that mean to your retirement?

The best I can tell, there are only three things the stock market can do.

The market can go up.

The market can go down.

The market can go sideways.

I do not believe the stock market will go steadily up in the next decade nor do I believe it will go steadily down. I believe we are in a sideways market. Does this mean the market goes sideways over the next 10 years as in a straight line like this?

Does it stay at its current value and never move for 10 years? Not at all. Rather it looks something like this:

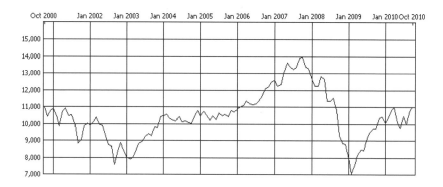

It goes up and down, but 10 years from now it will still be around the same value it is today. For a retiree this is trouble. If you had $100,000 in an account that lost 50% of its value, you would now have $50,000. However, to get back to $100,000 you don't need a 50% return. You need a 100% return. As a retiree, every time you lose money it takes a bigger percentage return to gain back what you have lost.

It is important to understand that before retirement we are in the "accumulation" stage of life. As we begin to save and accumulate money in our 20s and 30s, it really doesn't matter if the market is going up or down because we are *dollar cost averaging* (a system whereby you add a steady stream of money into your market investments each month regardless if the market is going up or down). Many times this is best represented by payroll deduction plans depositing into your account on a monthly basis. It can also be done through your bank on an automatic deduction from your bank account. This can still be profitable. Look at the example below.

Date	Amount Invested	Price per Share	Shares Purchased
January	$ 416.66	$ 33.21	12.55
February	$ 416.66	$ 35.70	11.67
March	$ 416.66	$ 34.83	11.96
April	$ 416.66	$ 32.10	12.98
May	$ 416.66	$ 33.71	12.36
June	$ 416.66	$ 35.08	11.88
July	$ 416.66	$ 29.04	14.35
August	$ 416.66	$ 28.17	14.79
September	$ 416.66	$ 27.92	14.92
October	$ 416.66	$ 25.83	16.13
November	$ 416.66	$ 26.42	15.77
December	$ 416.66	$ 28.18	14.79
Total	$ 4999.92	$ 30.46 avg.	164.15 shares

You can see that while the market is losing money, we are buying cheaper shares. Then as the market comes back, all of the shares we bought on sale now grow to a larger value and our portfolio as a whole benefits from this approach.

However once we retire, we no longer live in the "accumulation" stage of life. We now transfer into the "distribution" stage of life (the stage where we are no longer working and putting savings into an investment portfolio). This is something totally different. Yet, how many brokers give their clients the same advice in the distribution stage (their retirement years) as they do while they are younger and accumulating money during the accumulation stage?

When in the distribution stage of life, we are now depending on what we have saved to help provide our income needs. The main goal in the distribution stage/retirement years now becomes DON'T LOSE MONEY!

Losing money in the first 5 years of retirement could destroy your financial security!

Let's look at the Accumulation chart on page 37 and 38.

The chart is broken into two main columns. The only difference is the order of returns. The returns shown are purely hypothetical and not reflecting any actual returns of the market in the past.

The rates of return in the columns on the right are identical to the columns on the left. The only difference is I flipped the interest rates. Look at years 1 through 5 of each side. Now look at years 26 through 30 on each side. I simply reversed the order that rates of return earned based on the market over a 30 year period. The rates on the top of one side are now on the bottom of the other side of the chart.

The important fact is that the columns on the right now suffer some losses in the first 5 years due to negative markets, while the columns on the left during the first 5 years are all positive returns.

Accumulation
The "Upside" of the Mountain

		Illustrated Index Reversed		
Year	Age	Beginning Amount	Yearly Return	End of Year Value
1	65	$ 500,000	8%	$ 540,000
2	66	$ 540,000	-16%	$ 453,600
3	67	$ 453,600	-12%	$ 399,168
4	68	$ 399,168	27%	$ 506,943
5	69	$ 506,943	23%	$ 623,540
6	70	$ 623,540	-15%	$ 530,009
7	71	$ 530,009	22%	$ 646,611
8	72	$ 646,611	18%	$ 763,001
9	73	$ 763,001	-12%	$ 871,441
10	74	$ 871,441	20%	$ 805,729
11	75	$ 805,729	14%	$ 918,532
12	76	$ 918,532	-6%	$ 863,420
13	77	$ 863,420	18%	$ 1,018,832
14	78	$ 1,018,832	12%	$ 1,141,095
15	79	$ 1,141,095	-6%	$ 1,072,630
16	80	$ 1,072,630	23%	$ 1,319,335
17	81	$ 1,319,335	31%	$ 1,728,328
18	82	$ 1,728,328	-5%	$ 1,641,912
19	83	$ 1,641,912	11%	$ 1,822,522
20	84	$ 1,822,522	3%	$ 1,877,198
21	85	$ 1,877,198	23%	$ 2,308,953
22	86	$ 2,308,953	18%	$ 2,724,565
23	87	$ 2,724,565	-6%	$ 2,561,091
24	88	$ 2,561,091	18%	$ 3,022,087
25	89	$ 3,022,087	5%	$ 2,870,983
26	90	$ 2,870,983	19%	$ 3,416,470
27	91	$ 3,416,470	5%	$ 3,587,293
28	92	$ 3,587,293	11%	$ 3,981,896
29	93	$ 3,981,896	6%	$ 4,220,809
30	94	$ 4,220,809	18%	$ 4,980,555

Accumulation
The "Upside" of the Mountain

		Illustrated Index		
Year	Age	Beginning Amount	Yearly Return	End of Year Value
1	65	$ 500,000	18%	$ 590,000
2	66	$ 590,000	6%	$ 625,400
3	67	$ 625,194	11%	$ 694,194
4	68	$ 694,194	5%	$ 728,904
5	69	$ 728,904	19%	$ 867,395
6	70	$ 867,395	-5%	$ 824,026
7	71	$ 824,026	18%	$ 972,350
8	72	$ 972,350	-6%	$ 914,009
9	73	$ 914,009	18%	$ 1,078,531
10	74	$ 1,078,531	23%	$ 1,326,593
11	75	$ 1,326,593	3%	$ 1,366,391
12	76	$ 1,366,391	11%	$ 1,516,694
13	77	$ 1,516,694	-5%	$ 1,440,859
14	78	$ 1,440,859	31%	$ 1,887,525
15	79	$ 1,887,525	23%	$ 2,321,656
16	80	$ 2,321,656	-6%	$ 2,182,357
17	81	$ 2,182,357	12%	$ 2,444,240
18	82	$ 2,444,240	18%	$ 2,884,203
19	83	$ 2,884,203	-6%	$ 2,711,151
20	84	$ 2,711,151	14%	$ 3,090,712
21	85	$ 3,090,712	20%	$ 3,708,854
22	86	$ 3,708,854	-12%	$ 3,263,792
23	87	$ 3,263,792	18%	$ 3,851,274
24	88	$ 3,851,274	22%	$ 4,698,554
25	89	$ 4,698,554	-15%	$ 3,993,771
26	90	$ 3,993,771	23%	$ 4,912,339
27	91	$ 4,912,339	27%	$ 6,238,670
28	92	$ 6,238,670	-12%	$ 5,490,030
29	93	$ 5,490,030	-16%	$ 4,611,625
30	94	$ 4,611,625	8%	$ 4,980,555

You will notice that while accumulating assets, it has no impact whatsoever if and when you lose money in the market. You would end up with the same amount of money regardless of when the negative years occurred.

The important part of this is that when ACCUMULATING AS-SETS in your younger years you can afford the risk of the market better.

LOSING MONEY WHILE IN RETIREMENT CAN DESTROY YOUR ECONOMIC FUTURE.

Now look at the next chart. The "Distribution" chart on pages 40 and 41.

You will notice virtually the same chart and rates of return as on the accumulation chart. The only difference is that you now may need to depend on your assets for income in retirement. I have used an example of this person pulling out $35,000 per year of income or 7% of his portfolio value.

As you can see in the "yearly returns" column where there were no losses in the first 5 years, there is no negative impact. The investor's assets did the job and provided for him or her entire retirement. Now look at the "yearly returns" column on the next graph, where the market loses in two of the first 5 years. This person is broke at the age of 82.

The only difference was losing money in the first 5 years while taking a distribution.

The point of this is that when DISTRIBUTING ASSETS in your retirement years you may not be able to afford the risk of a buy and hold strategy in the stock market.

In the next chapter, I will begin to share how you can be in total control of how your money is invested and identify a way to better communicate with your financial professional as to what you would like your portfolio to look like.

Distribution/Withdrawals
The "Upside" of the Mountain

Illustrated Index					
Year	Age	Beginning Amount	Yearly Return	Annual Withdrawal	End of Year Value
1	65	$ 500,000	18%	$35,000	$ 555,250
2	66	$ 555,250	6%	$36,050	$ 552,250
3	67	$ 552,250	11%	$37,132	$ 575,866
4	68	$ 575,866	5%	$38,245	$ 566,414
5	69	$ 566,414	19%	$39,393	$ 634,640
6	70	$ 634,640	-5%	$40,575	$ 562,333
7	71	$ 562,333	18%	$41,792	$ 621,761
8	72	$ 621,761	-6%	$43,048	$ 541,410
9	73	$ 541,410	18%	$44,337	$ 594,527
10	74	$ 594,527	23%	$45,667	$ 685,601
11	75	$ 685,601	3%	$47,037	$ 659,132
12	76	$ 659,132	11%	$48,448	$ 683,188
13	77	$ 683,188	-5%	$49,902	$ 599,127
14	78	$ 599,127	31%	$51,399	$ 733,458
15	79	$ 733,458	23%	$52,941	$ 849,213
16	80	$ 849,213	-6%	$54,529	$ 743,731
17	81	$ 743,731	12%	$56,165	$ 776,814
18	82	$ 776,814	18%	$57,850	$ 858,791
19	83	$ 858,791	-6%	$59,585	$ 747,678
20	84	$ 747,678	14%	$61,373	$ 790,980
21	85	$ 790,980	20%	$63,214	$ 885,963
22	86	$ 885,963	-12%	$66,110	$ 714,537
23	87	$ 714,537	18%	$67,064	$ 776,090
24	88	$ 776,090	22%	$69,076	$ 877,754
25	89	$ 877,754	-15%	$71,148	$ 674,943
26	90	$ 674,943	23%	$73,282	$ 756,898
27	91	$ 756,898	27%	$75,481	$ 885,780
28	92	$ 885,780	-12%	$77,745	$ 701,741
29	93	$ 701,741	-16%	$80,077	$ 509,385
30	94	$ 509,385	8%	$82,480	$ 467,656

Distribution/Withdrawals
The "Downside" of the Mountain

Illustrated Index Reversed				
Year	Age	Beginning Amount	Yearly Return	Annual Withdrawal	End of Year Value
1	65	$ 500,000	8%	$35,000	$ 505,000
2	66	$ 505,000	-16%	$36,050	$ 388.150
3	67	$ 388.150	-12%	$37,132	$ 304,441
4	68	$ 304,441	27%	$38,245	$ 348.394
5	69	$ 348.394	23%	$39,393	$ 389.132
6	70	$ 389.132	-15%	$40,575	$ 290,187
7	71	$ 290,187	22%	$41,792	$ 312,237
8	72	$ 312,237	18%	$43,048	$ 325,394
9	73	$ 325,394	-12%	$44,337	$ 242,010
10	74	$ 242,010	20%	$45,667	$ 244,745
11	75	$ 244,745	14%	$47,037	$ 231,972
12	76	$ 231,972	-6%	$48,448	$ 169,605
13	77	$ 169,605	18%	$49,902	$ 150,233
14	78	$ 150,233	12%	$51,399	$ 116,862
15	79	$ 116,862	-6%	$52,941	$ 56,909
16	80	$ 56,909	23%	$54,529	$ 15,470
17	81	$ 15,470	31%	$56,165	$ (35,899)
18	82	$ (35,899)	-5%	$57,850	$ (91,954)
19	83	$ (91,954)	11%	$59,585	$ (161,654)
20	84	$ (161,654)	34%	$61,373	$ (227,877)
21	85	$ (227,877)	23%	$63,214	$ (343,502)
22	86	$ (343,502)	18%	$66,110	$ (470,443)
23	87	$ (470,443)	-6%	$67,064	$ (509,280)
24	88	$ (509,280)	18%	$69,076	$ (670,026)
25	89	$ (670,026)	-5%	$71,148	$ (707,672)
26	90	$ (707,672)	19%	$73,282	$ (915,412)
27	91	$ (915,412)	5%	$75,481	$ (1,036,663)
28	92	$ (1,036,663)	11%	$77,745	$ (1,228,442)
29	93	$ (1,228,442)	6%	$80,077	$ (1,382,225)
30	94	$ (1,382,225)	18%	$82,480	$ (1,714,506)

CHAPTER 5

Questions That Will Change Your Life!

In order to do this properly, I will pretend that we are actually sitting in front of each other and I'll be asking you questions. These would be the same questions I would ask someone new to our office. I will be giving you some hints and tips along the way. It's my hope that the questions will help you develop clarity surrounding your retirement goals and dreams. The key to your retirement lays not in stocks, bonds and mutual funds. It does not lay in how good you are at picking the right investment. The key to your financial future lays solely and totally in the strategies that you implement and can come from completing this form of a question and answer time.

Here we go then.

What specifically brought you into visit with us today?

Your answer to this question should be based upon what concerns you today. In other words, as you look at your financial portfolio and your advisors (financial planner, CPA, tax practitioner, or attorney), what is it that concerns you today? What is it that caused you to seek out help from another person like myself? Take a moment before you read on and fill in the blank space below and answer that question.

_____

_____

_____

_____

_____

The things that concern me the most are:

_____

_____

_____

_____

Specifically, how does it make you feel knowing that these concerns and problems are present?

_____

_____

_____

_____

If we could resolve these problems for you, how would that change your outlook on your retirement?

_____

_____

_____

_____

_____

Describe the ideal retirement for you and your spouse.

Where will you live?

_____

_____

Will you have one home or two?

_____

_____

Are there any hobbies that you or your spouse enjoy that you just haven't gotten around to because of time demands?

If so, what are they?

_____

_____

_____

_____

Would you like to travel?

If there were three locations that you definitely want to go to during your retirement, where would they be?

_____

_____

_____

_____

Do you have any other goals or dreams for your retirement that you would like to list?

_____

_____

_____

_____

Do you own a home?   Yes   No

If yes, what is the current market value of your home?

$ _____

What is the mortgage balance on that home?

$ _____

Equity on home? (value minus mortgage)

$ _____

Do you own any other real estate?   Yes   No

If yes, what is the combined current market value of all other real estate owned?

$ _____

What is its mortgage balance, if any?

$ _____

What is your equity? (value minus mortgage)

$ _____

What is your cost basis for all other real estate?

$ _____

Do you have a pension?   Yes   No

If yes, what is the monthly amount you receive/will receive each month?

Yours $ _____

Spouses $ _____

Does it reduce at either spouse's death?   Yes   No

If yes, to what amount?

Yours $ _____

Spouses $ _____

What is your date of birth?

Yours _____

Spouses _____

What is your current or projected Social Security income per month?

Yours $ _____ (current)

           $ _____ (projected at age 66/67)

Spouses $ _____ (current)

           $ _____ (projected at age 66/67)

Do you have any other sources of monthly or annual income?

    Yes   No

If yes, list your other sources of income

Source: _____

$ _____ per month/year

Source: _____

$ _____ per month/year

Source: _____

$ _____ per month/year

Are you currently retired?   Yes   No

If no, how many years until you plan to do so?

How many retirement years would you like to plan for?
(I realize no one knows the date they may die but at least list how long you want to make sure you are covered with income and assets)

Number of years for retirement to last? _____

What income do you feel you would need to be able to retire in TODAY'S DOLLARS? (please be realistic)

Income needed per year (after tax) $ _____

Did you claim any interest income last year?   Yes   No

If yes, how much? (found on line 8A of your tax return)

Interest income $ _____

Did you claim any "ordinary dividends" on your tax return for last year?   Yes   No

If yes, how much? (found on line 9A of your tax return)

Ordinary Dividends: $ _____

What was the Social Security income listed on your tax return last year, if any? (found on line 20A of your tax return)

Social Security income last year? $ _____

Did you claim any of your Social Security payments as taxable income this past year? (found on line 20B of your tax return)

Social Security income claimed last year: $ _____

How much life insurance do you carry?
(If you are still working, do not claim insurance that you will lose once retired. Only count insurance that can follow you into retirement)

Total death benefit amount

Yours $ _____

Spouses $ _____

Cost of all insurance policies per year

Yours $ _____

Spouses $ _____

Current cash value of all policies, if any

Yours $ _____

Spouses $ _____

Please note that you should work with your advisor to identify the need, or lack thereof, for life insurance in your retirement years. There are many issues to consider other than paying for final expenses. You may need to cover some estate tax issues. You could lose a pension on the death of the first spouse, as well as some Social Security income and need to replace it. You may have charitable gifts that you would like to make. You may want some assets in trust for the benefit of your children or a special needs child. Make sure you consult a professional life insurance agent or your financial advisor to discuss these important issues.

If you are married this next question needs to be answered by both husband and wife. Answer independently of how the other person would respond. Don't worry about what your spouse's answer might be. Be honest with your own.

On a scale of 1 to 10, with 10 being your willingness to take risk on your investments and 1 indicating you don't like risk of any kind, circle the number you would be?

You   1 2 3 4 5 6 7 8 9 10

Spouse   1 2 3 4 5 6 7 8 9 10

While I love my children, I am only worried about providing for my (and spouse's) retirement.   Yes   No

While supporting my retirement is my number one concern, it would be important to me to leave a financial legacy to my children as well.   Yes   No

Do you have a will?   Yes   No

When was the last year it was updated? _____

Do you have a trust?   Yes   No

When was the last year it was updated? _____

Do you plan, or would you like to leave any, charitable gifts (if you could do so without hurting your retirement or family)? These could be organizations that mean something to you such as your church, missions, American Cancer Society, or other similar organization.   Yes   No

List the names of organizations that might be important to you.

_____

_____

_____

_____

_____

_____

If I had the privilege of serving you as a client and 3 years from now we were sitting together, what would need to have happened for you to be satisfied and happy with our professional relationship together?

_____

_____

_____

_____

_____

_____

_____

_____

_____

_____

_____

_____

_____

_____

_____

_____

Your Current Investments:

Account #1

First name ONLY on account

_____

This investment is with (i.e.: Merrill Lynch, Morgan Stanley, American Funds, Scottrade, etc.)

_____

The title on the account is (circle one)

JTWROS   Single name trust   IRA

Roth IRA   Co. Retirement Plan

Total value of all stocks, bonds, mutual funds, and variable annuities ONLY within the account

$ _____

Total value of all "alternative investments" (REITS (real estate investment trusts), second homes or property you own, gold, silver, equipment leasing programs) within the account

$ _____

Total value of all guaranteed investments (bank accounts, fixed annuities, fixed or equity index annuities, federally backed bonds) within the account

$ _____

Account #2 (if needed)

First name ONLY on account

_____

This investment is with (i.e.: Merrill Lynch, Morgan Stanley, American Funds, Scottrade, etc.)

_____

The title on the account is (circle one)

JTWROS   Single name trust   IRA

Roth IRA   Co. Retirement Plan

Total value of all stocks, bonds, mutual funds, and variable annuities ONLY within the account

$ _____

Total value of all "alternative investments" (REITS (real estate investment trusts), second homes or property you own, gold, silver, equipment leasing programs) within the account

$ _____

Total value of all guaranteed investments (bank accounts, fixed annuities, fixed or equity index annuities, federally backed bonds) within the account

$ _____

Account #3 (if needed)

First name ONLY on account

_____

This investment is with (i.e.: Merrill Lynch, Morgan Stanley, American Funds, Scottrade, etc.)

_____

The title on the account is (circle one)

JTWROS   Single name trust   IRA

Roth IRA   Co. Retirement Plan

Total value of all stocks, bonds, mutual funds, and variable annuities ONLY within the account

$ _____

Total value of all "alternative investments" (REITS (real estate investment trusts), second homes or property you own, gold, silver, equipment leasing programs) within the account

$ _____

Total value of all guaranteed investments (bank accounts, fixed annuities, fixed or equity index annuities, federally backed bonds) within the account

$ _____

Account #4 (if needed)

First name ONLY on account

_____

This investment is with (i.e.: Merrill Lynch, Morgan Stanley, American Funds, Scottrade, etc.)

_____

The title on the account is (circle one)

JTWROS   Single name trust   IRA

Roth IRA   Co. Retirement Plan

Total value of all stocks, bonds, mutual funds, and variable annuities ONLY within the account

$ _____

Total value of all "alternative investments" (REITS (real estate investment trusts), second homes or property you own, gold, silver, equipment leasing programs) within the account

$ _____

Total value of all guaranteed investments (bank accounts, fixed annuities, fixed or equity index annuities, federally backed bonds) within the account

$ _____

Account #5 (if needed)

First name ONLY on account

_____

This investment is with (i.e.: Merrill Lynch, Morgan Stanley, American Funds, Scottrade, etc.)

_____

The title on the account is (circle one)

JTWROS   Single name trust   IRA

Roth IRA   Co. Retirement Plan

Total value of all stocks, bonds, mutual funds, and variable annuities ONLY within the account

$ _____

Total value of all "alternative investments" (REITS (real estate investment trusts), second homes or property you own, gold, silver, equipment leasing programs) within the account

$ _____

Total value of all guaranteed investments (bank accounts, fixed annuities, fixed or equity index annuities, federally backed bonds) within the account

$ _____

Account #6 (if needed)

First name ONLY on account

_____

This investment is with (i.e.: Merrill Lynch, Morgan Stanley, American Funds, Scottrade, etc.)

_____

The title on the account is (circle one)

JTWROS   Single name trust   IRA

Roth IRA   Co. Retirement Plan

Total value of all stocks, bonds, mutual funds, and variable annuities ONLY within the account

$ _____

Total value of all "alternative investments" (REITS (real estate investment trusts), second homes or property you own, gold, silver, equipment leasing programs) within the account

$ _____

Total value of all guaranteed investments (bank accounts, fixed annuities, fixed or equity index annuities, federally backed bonds) within the account

$ _____

Has your advisor asked you these questions before? If so that's a great start.

Unfortunately I find that many advisors never really dive this deep into your financial life. Yet, after some brief questions, he/she can begin to recommend investments to you. In reality, they are investment salespeople. They can sometimes be likened to a car salesman (no offense to car salesman intended). A car salesperson may begin by asking what you are looking for. What kind of payments (risk) you are willing to take. What you wanted to spend on a car (or how much you want to invest) and then boom! Have I got the right car... oops... investment for you!

Your retirement is far too important to leave this to a salesman who may or may not be with the firm in 2 years, or who doesn't care enough to take the time to dig and make sure they create not just some investment ideas, but as you will learn and most importantly, help you identify or create for you strategies that can help meet your goals and dreams.

I hope this does not represent your advisor. If you feel you have a good advisor, take the answers to these questions to him/her and have another meeting to review and make sure your investments and strategies match your goals.

Finally, if you would like help in formulating a Red, Blue, Green analysis for you to take to your advisor, you can contact my office and we will send it along for your advisors review.

Here's to your future, a future that results in reaching your dreams and goals.

CHAPTER 6

Red, Blue, Green
Putting You in Control

Jack Nicholas is undisputedly one of the greatest golfers of all time. There is a current golfer who seems to be challenging Jack for this title and of course that would be Tiger Woods. Though Tiger has had his struggles of late with his image, no one can deny his greatness on the golf course. Time will tell if he can come back and return to his once level of superiority.

Let me ask you a question. What's more important, Tiger Woods or his golf clubs? I bet I could run out to Kmart and buy a set of the most inexpensive golf clubs and give them to Tiger Woods and give or take two or three strokes, he could possibly golf close to as well as he would with his own clubs. You see the magic to Tiger Woods and Jack Nicholas is not their clubs. It's their swing! On countless occasions I've had the ability to golf with friends and associates only to find that they spent $300-$400 maybe even $500 on a brand-new driver because it promised that they could hit it further. And interestingly, their score never seems to change. They still stayed in the same range of scores they usually fell within. Why? It's not about the clubs. It's about their swing.

When looking at your financial investments, those are really the clubs in your investment portfolio. If you're looking to get a great return on a long-term investment, you want to hit the ball far down the course and get as much distance as you can. In golf, this would be your driver. Drivers can hit the ball the farthest, but can also cause the ball to go off target the most. If you wanted just a little chip shot up onto the green, you might pull out your sand wedge or your pitching wedge. Why? You usually are far more accurate with the shorter clubs. This would mean less distance, but far less risk of sending the ball off in the wrong direction.

Golf is a game of strategy and skill. If you don't use the right clubs for the right distance, you increase your risk of a poor score/result.

In building a portfolio for your retirement years, it's the same thing. The only difference is instead of clubs, you choose your investments. For a long drive, you would go to a higher risk stock or mutual fund that is more risky but could possibly provide long-term growth. A bond might represent, at times, a little less risk, but would not take your ball (growth) as far. However, just like golf, you need more than clubs; you need the right strategy (the right swing).

When taking lessons one time the golf pro asked me what iron I felt the most comfortable using. I told him my pitching wedge, which I usually hit about 110 yards. He then recommended that when coming down the fairway on a par five, if after my first shot I had 250 yards to go, instead of going for the green on my second shot (which at that distance I'd have little hope of achieving) to go for a 140 yard shot instead. This would call for my 7 or 8 iron, which I would be far more accurate with than a 3 wood, and my goal would be to lay up my second shot 110 yards from the green. This then would leave me at the perfect distance for the club I am most confident in (my pitching wedge). By using the wedge on my third shot, I'd have a much better chance of getting the ball closer to the pin and thereby have a better chance for a birdie on my fourth shot. That is a "strategy" to get a better score in golf. In the same way strategy is a major part of the game of investing.

In investing, if you don't have a strategy of your own, then you end up turning to a professional, as you should, for help in creating the right "customized strategy" for you. An investment advisor can be a coach for your investment strategy just as a golf pro is for a golfing strategy.

Do you just go out and start buying investments (swinging your investment clubs) or would it be smart to consider getting lessons along the way? Trying to secure your retirement without a strategy and without the right coach is like trying to lower your score by just continuing to swing away with any club in your bag. Remember practice DOESN'T make perfect; perfect practice helps you get closer to your goals.

Fortunately or unfortunately, depending on how you look at it, there are many financial coaches available to choose from. But not all financial coaches are the right ones for you. In the last chapter, I will address how you can find the right investment coach for your portfolio. For now though, let's talk about how financial advisors and brokers can let you down.

So now you realize you need a strategy and you need a financial coach. Your goal is to find a financial coach who will help you design a plan for your ideal retirement. However, you may not be sure how to get there or what investments (clubs) you will need. Most importantly, you need to develop the proper swing (be educated) so YOU can better judge the investments (clubs) you will need at each step of the plan and depending on the market conditions (weather). Your number one goal is to reach your goals with THE LEAST AMOUNT OF RISK POSSIBLE (you want to lower your score). You want a safer approach to your goals and the right strategies to do so. You want to **secure** your retirement.

What do many advisors do? They tell you about this really awesome stock or mutual fund that can hit the ball 350 yards, and, of course, they say with very little risk (just like on the TV commercials for that new driver). In investing terms they don't talk about your strategy or needs for your retirement goals. As a matter of fact, they don't even talk about setting goals or objectives, rather they tell you about the latest and greatest stock or investment that will help you get a 12-15% return (hit the ball farther down the fairway) instead of a 10% return (you can get an extra 20 yards) with this new investment (club).

Many advisors believe that it's all about the rate of return. They believe the advisor who gets you the best return (the one who can teach you to hit the ball the farthest) is the one that wins. But what about my overall strategy, you say? If they didn't ask you about your goals and then help you develop strategies to attain them, they really are nothing more than a salesman who makes a commission on what you buy. They figure if they can sell you an investment that has a better rate of return than the one you have now, you're going to jump ship, and you're going to buy their investment. Ladies and gentlemen, please don't fall prey to advisors/salesman trying to sell you a fancier investment/golf club.

First and foremost, you must identify what you want. Once we have a clear picture of what you want, we now have the swing down for the retirement you desire. The only remaining factor then is to develop a strategy that when applied with your swing will help you reach your retirement goals. Once the goals and strategies are laid out, we can then make sure we are choosing the right investment and more accurately predict where we are going to end up. But you must have the swing/strategy not to just pick clubs based on someone else's opinion of what those investments may or may not achieve regardless of your plans.

Unfortunately, helping you identify your goals and strategies is a custom thing for each individual reading this book. As much as

I would like to help each of you with your individual strategies, it is impossible to do. The public today is bombarded with so called professional advisors on the radio and in print who lead you to believe their advice is the right advice. *The right advice can only be determined on a one-on-one basis*, not over the radio. What might be the right thing to do for a 35 year old client can be the worst thing a retiree can do. Yet there they are giving advice to everyone listening to the radio or reading their magazines as if it doesn't matter what your goals and strategies are; their advice is always right. **WRONG!**

For now, I would like to teach you how to never fall prey again to the wrong advisor and end up with more risk than you would intend to take or desire. This is a system I created and have used for the past 10 years that has more safely guided our clients through the financial storms of the decade from 2000 through 2012. The system is called "Red, Blue, Green."

For the rest of this book, I will refer to Red, Blue and Green as RBG. RBG is a system that will help you know how much risk you are taking and put you back in control of that risk instead of what your advisor thinks is the right amount of risk.

Earlier, I spoke of clients coming into our offices stating they told their advisor they didn't want as much risk as they previously had. Yet they carried higher degrees of risk. Why? Because the advisors idea of risk and he clients idea of risk can be worlds apart.

Let's see how the colors can help you determine your risk.

Red Money

Red money investments are defined as the most popular investments that are tied to Wall Street. This would mean stocks, bonds and mutual funds for most of America. While there can be other investments that would qualify for this, they are seldom seen or used by most advisors. I base this on my 29 years of experience in looking at countless statements from potentially new clients in our offices. If you did have Wall Street investments that are not in these three general categories, you probably wouldn't be reading this book.

Blue Money

Blue money represents investments that are often referred to as "Alternative Investments". These are many times things like Real Estate Trusts (REITS), equipment leasing programs, precious metals, like gold and silver, High Grade Rare Coins, and collectibles.

Over the last decade of 2000-2009, these investments have been a critical part of our client's investment portfolios. Yet, we seldom see many of these (if any) in potential client's accounts when they visit us. The key to this part of RBG is it can help create a portion of the portfolio that has historically created good income or a low correlation to the stock market.

Green Money

Green Money quite simply is accounts that come with a guarantee of some sort. They are either backed by the FDIC, the Legal Reserve System which is supported by the insurance industry, or insurance companies themselves. To put it simply, these are investments in your portfolio that have guarantees to not lose your principal (and sometimes even your earnings).

Why Red, Blue, Green?

Not everyone learns best through visual illustrations, some people learn better through hearing as an example. However, I have never met anyone yet, that when using RBG to show them the current diversification and risk in their portfolio, didn't find it a major benefit in helping them make better investment decisions.

Let's look at what a RBG chart would look like for a typical person or couple coming into our office.

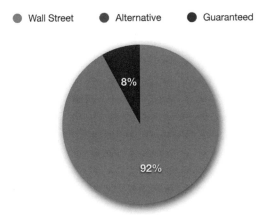

As you can see, this graph is mostly made up of Wall Street investments (Red). Is it any wonder why when 2008 came along this sample client lost up to 50% or more of their investments? In 2008, the stock market lost 37%. I had some new potential clients who had lost 25 to 30% with their broker and others who lost up to 80% of their portfolio! Either way, if you are within 5 years of retirement or older, that is catastrophic!

Once a prospective client sees the amount of red in their chart, they almost instantly say, "I didn't want that much risk!" Now, they can be in control of the risk they carry. How? Because they can see a picture. You see the advisor did what he or she thought was best. However, their idea of risk and the clients can be miles apart. By viewing your portfolio in colors, you can identify how well diversified you are and therefore more likely to handle a market downturn.

Following is a chart that would indicate a far better diversified portfolio.

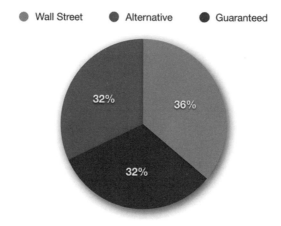

At this point some of you are now saying "Hold on. Curt! I have all of my money in bonds. Wouldn't that count for great diversification? Yet you show bonds in red money."

The Biggest Mistake of the Past Decade

In my opinion, the biggest mistake of the past decade has been advisors giving the same advice from 2000 to present as they did from 1985-1999. Let me explain why bonds may be a concern for many investors over the next 5 to 8 years and possibly beyond.

Do you remember what interest rates were doing in 1981? As I state earlier and sourced it, inflation over a two year period was up over 24%. According to analysis by Mortgage-X, the highest certificate of deposit rates (for 3-month CDs) occurred in 1981. That year, rates reached a high of 16.691 percent, with an average rate for the year of 14.897 percent. Measures of longer- or shorter-duration CD rates also show the highest CD rates in 1981. You might be thinking "If I ever see rates like that again, I'm throwing all of my money in the bank!" WAIT! If inflation was running higher than the rate you are might be earning in your CD you're losing money each year! I'm not saying don't buy a 16% CD. I'm saying that is all green money and if that's all you have, then you will not be keeping up with the cost of living and instead be slowly sliding toward poverty. Again, you must have balance indicated by proper diversification through RBG.

Now let's go back to my point. What has happened to interest rates from the early 80's to present (2011)? They have for all intents and purposes done nothing but go down as seen in the mortgage rate history below;

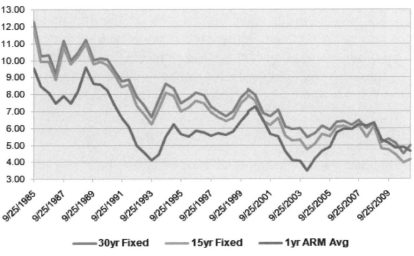

(www.bankrate.com)

Question: As interest rates go down, what happens to the value of bonds? They go UP! From 1981 to 2012, bonds may have helped your portfolio against stock market falls. The reason is many of the bonds you were holding (not all...like high yields) were going up in value due to falling interest rates thereby helping protect against some of your losses in stocks.

Next question: where are interest rates today? Answer: At the lowest point in history for any person who is alive today.

Final question: If interest rates are this low, what are the odds of them going down much further (if at all) versus the odds of going up over the next 4 to 6 years? I would say the chances are excellent they will be going up! As we just learned, when rates go down, bonds go up. Therefore, if you truly believe as I do rates will be going up then bonds must go down.

That is why bonds are listed with all of the other Wall Street investments in the red. I personally believe bonds will be far more risky in the years ahead than at any time in the last 30 years. Now if stocks are losing while interest rates are slowly rising (which means bonds are also losing), where does that leave your portfolio? Of course, some bonds will lose more than others. However, the future rise in interest rates will be a sinking tide that will take all bonds with it to some degree or another.

The Problem

The problem is that most advisors today are still giving advice as if we were somewhere in 1981 to 1999. If that is your advisor, here is how you can better prepare yourself and not be so dependent on him or her alone.

Step #1:

Grab a sheet of paper and create three columns. Title each column as either Red, Blue, or Green. Go through all of your investments and put the name and dollar value of each investment or asset you own in the proper column based on my description of each above. Do not include your primary residence value or life insurance death benefits (cash values are okay) as you can't depend on them for income. Once complete, add up each column and identify the percentage of investments in each category. To identify the percentage, grab a calculator. Take the total value of the red column and divide it by the total value of all three columns.

Example:

Total of all three columns = $1,152,345

Total of red money = $932,131

$932,131 divided by $1,152,345 = 81% red money.

Do this for each column and you will now see how well diversified your portfolio is compared to just being diversified in Wall Street.

Most of the time, it is not unusual for us to see prospective clients without any Blue Money. In the case just illustrated, it would most likely be 81% red, 0% blue and 19% green (and all of the green money would most likely be in the bank at today's rate of just 1%).

This is NOT proper diversification and now you know that. If you are working with an advisor who understands RBG, then you can now communicate with him or her in a manner that you will both understand YOUR wishes and not just their opinions.

On many occasions, I have had clients call me up before their quarterly reviews. They might say something like, "I was looking at my portfolio and I'm not sure I have enough green money. When I come in, can you be prepared to share ideas with me on other investments that might fit into the green category and be right for me?" Now that's putting you, the client, back in charge!

When you find an advisor who understands this concept, they can better help educate you and create a balanced portfolio that will help you achieve your financial goals. If I know a client must average 5% in their portfolio to reach their goals, I can then educate and guide them into making smart RBG investments that together will MORE SAFELY help them achieve this 5% objective.

Finally, once a RBG portfolio is properly achieved, it cannot be considered done or complete forever. Ongoing rebalancing between the RBG is critical to make sure you stay on path with your objectives. In addition, as economics change, your advisor may recommend changing the percentage of allocation to each category in order to maintain the ability to achieve the pre-determined goals you selected at the beginning of your relationship.

Next we'll discuss forming your own personal pension plan.

CHAPTER 7

Forming Your Own Personal Pension Plan and Guaranteeing Your Income for Life

Are you ready for a good laugh? When I was in high school, I was far from being an honor roll student. I always waited until the last minute to get my homework and other school projects done. Both of my parents worked hard (not for financial gain as much as just making sure the bills got paid) and therefore weren't always there to help me with my homework. One time, I was told that I had a term paper that had to be handed in by the end of the semester. We were given virtually any subject we wished to write the paper on. Here's where it gets funny… I chose to do my paper on "The Brain." Not just one area of the brain, not just one function of the brain, but the **entire brain!** Talk about biting off more than you can chew! How can you describe in complete and thorough detail everything there is concerning the brain in one term paper? To make matters worse, I, of course, delayed beginning my work until the week it was due. After many hours and sleepless nights, many pots of coffee and research (some nights literally staying up all night), I turned in my paper and did better on the grade than you are probably guessing… I got a D.

My point is: there was far too much to know to be able to do justice in one term paper on the brain! What's that got to do with your retirement?

The world of investing is far too broad and complex for someone who is untrained in investing and economics (as well as those who spent their career in the investment world) to understand enough to secure and guarantee their economic future.

I have one client who I will refer to as Bill. Bill has most of his retirement assets with my firm and counts on us to direct his way financially. However, Bill has about $100,000 in his personal account outside our firm because he wants to do some of his own investing and believes he can earn a better return by doing so. Bill spends 4 to 6 hours per day at his computer following his portfolio and researching his investments. I will admit, he is doing quite well (slightly better than what we have achieved). However, it comes at a great price. Bill's wife constantly tells me of his sleepless nights, worries and fears about his investments. I'm fearful the stress could shorten Bills life! I can think of a lot of ways to spend the 4 to 6 hours per day that Bill is doing rather than in front of a computer worrying about my stocks!

There is one investment that seems to be appropriate for many people depending on their age and financial goals. Let me caution that it is not the ONLY investment that should be in your portfolio, but could warrant your interest, depending on your rate of return needs and risk tolerance level among other things.

It is a green money account called a "Fixed Index Annuity" (sometimes referred to as an Equity Index Annuity). In this chapter, it will be my objective to explain in general how a Fixed Index Annuity works.

With so much uncertainty today, the FIA comes with some guarantees by the issuing insurance company, most important of which (depending on the options chosen) can provide an income for the rest of your life regardless of market conditions. There are (as with any investment) some drawbacks to annuity that we will address as we look more closely at them. To make it more efficient, I will refer to the Fixed Index Annuity for the rest of this chapter as an FIA.

You will find most stock brokers dislike this type of investment and will seldom recommend it. There are two reasons for this. First, their broker/dealer (the company they work for) refuses to allow them to sell it. Not because it is a bad investment. Rather it's because of the second reason brokers won't recommend this annuity; they can't trade it and make commissions or trail fees (ongoing annual commissions) off of it the way they can on stock and bond portfolios. Also, once you have invested in an FIA investment, you no longer need a professional to manage the money every year. This is because it is guaranteed against loss of principal or earnings by the insurance company and all management of assets is handled by the company at no risk to the investor. This cost the broker/dealers a profit. Whether you know it or not, I believe they are not in business to help you as much as they are to make money.

I myself am a licensed stock broker just like many other registered representatives. I too recommend managed money accounts and other securities to my clients. However, why wouldn't they also recommend as part of a complete and well balanced investment portfolio, a portion into a guaranteed investment that can create a pension like income for their clients that can never run out for the life of the client? I can only think of one reason...it doesn't make them enough money. They can't constantly trade it and make commissions each time.

Each broker will give their reasons why they may or may not think FIA's may be a good investment for you. My goal is to share what I see as some of the key factors of FIAs and let you be the judge of whether or not they are the right fit for part of your portfolio.

Before we begin explaining the general basics of how these investments work, it is important for you to understand that there are dozens of insurance companies selling these investments and each company can have 3 to 10 various forms of FIAs. I can in no way offer a company name or specifics for each FIA available, that will have to be left to your professional financial advisor to guide you to the one that he or she feels is the best fit for your objectives and goals.

How Do FIAs Differ from Other Forms of Annuities?

Many times when people come into our office, and we mention the word annuity, we can get an initial negative response. I believe this is due to either false information or a misunderstanding of what they are and how they work, or a commission motivated broker sold them an inappropriate one. There are two major types of annuities: **fixed** and **variable**. Most of the negativity we hear surrounds the idea of a variable annuity.

Variable Annuities (VAs)

Variable annuities, with the exception of a fixed option or money market fund, are Red money accounts. Basically they are nothing more than a group of mutual funds held in a separate account by the insurance company and wrapped in a shell called an annuity. The reason for this is that a traditional mutual fund is a taxable investment. However, the separate account that holds mutual funds inside of a VA makes it a tax-deferred way to own mutual funds. While definitely an advantage, it comes with some concerns. First, the fees within a VA can be quite high. Typically, you would see costs in the range of at least 2-3% per year. This is why many advisors (and I agree with them) teach that it may not be wise to put IRA money inside of a VA. You can usually buy the same mutual fund in an IRA outside of a VA as what you might find in a VA. Therefore there is sometimes little reason to put IRA money into a VA since the IRA is already tax-deferred. Also, with the exceptions stated above, you would then save paying the enormously high fees that a VA charges. Because VA's are mostly Red money, it is a Wall Street investment and therefore can lose money.

One of the most misleading things I see many brokers do is to sell a rider on the VA called an income rider and mislead the investor as to what the rider does. Please understand that there is nothing wrong with purchasing an income rider in a VA account. Under the right conditions and with proper explanation, the rider can be a wise choice. The problem comes in when the market falls and a client gets their statement. They call their broker to express their concern over the losses they just incurred and the broker tells them they are looking at the wrong number and points them to the rider value. Why is this misleading? The rider value in a VA is a second line item *that is only of value if the annuitant (usually the investor) decides to take his or her money out over time.* If the investor says I want all the money now, they would get the actual value of the account which could be worth far less than the rider value and certainly could be less than what they put into the account.

So remember, a VA is Red money that does not guarantee your principal or earnings. It is very expensive due to fees of 2-3%. Also, VA's (as all annuities) come with a time commitment and a withdrawal charge if you take out your **entire account** early. However, you can usually take out 10% each year without a charge. Most VA's time commitment ranges from 3 to 9 years. If your number one concern is growth, and you can settle for an income instead of getting your principal back, then these could be an investment you may want to investigate.

Fixed Annuities

Fixed annuities come in two forms, **fixed index** and **fixed interest** annuities.

Fixed interest annuities act very much like a CD in a bank. CD's however, are insured by the FDIC, whereas Fixed Annuities are guaranteed by the insurance company and an insurance industry form called the Legal Reserve. Please note the legal reserve is not a federal entity or backed by the government. Rather it is an industry guaranty.

With a fixed annuity, you invest with the insurance company and receive a fixed rate of interest for that year. Though the initial fixed rate is guaranteed for a time, the rate of interest you receive can usually change during the entire time you hold it as rates change. Since we are currently in a low interest rate environment, fixed annuities can be a good choice. This is because as interest rates go up, there is a good chance that your rate of return will change each year and increase with them. Though the rate is guaranteed for a year at a time, when you invest in a fixed annuity you are investing in a "time deposit." This means you buy them for usually 3 to 5 years or more. If you pull out early, there could be an "early withdrawal" charge for not honoring the time you committed to. However, fixed annuities do something CDs don't. Each year you are typically allowed to pull out up to 10% of the balance of your account without a penalty charge. This offers some flexibility. When you combine this with the potential of a rising interest rate as rates in the market place increase, it can be considered a good conservative investment.

Fixed Index Annuities (FIAs)

The most important aspect of a FIA is that it is guaranteed against loss (unlike a VA). Your principal is guaranteed by two factors. First, it is guaranteed by the insurance company that issues the annuity. Secondly, it is supported by the legal reserve system as mentioned before. Again, it is important to know the legal reserve is not a federally backed program. Rather, it is a program supported by the entire insurance industry. If you have your money with company "A" and they someday got in trouble financially, then the other member companies within the legal reserve system would step in and honor your money. The only way you can lose your money in an FIA annuity is if the entire insurance industry went broke at the same time. So, while not government guaranteed or FDIC backed, the FIA comes with a very strong set of its own guarantees.

Insurance Company Ratings

Since your fixed annuities value is guaranteed by the issuing company, it can be important to check the ratings of a company you might consider investing with. This can be done by going to www.ambest.com.

How does the FIA work?

While FIA returns are tied to market performance, your investment is never actually subject to market losses. Let's assume you invested $100,000 on November 28th. During the first year of your investment (November 28th until November 28th of the following year), if the stock market has a gain, you could have a profit. However, if the stock market loses money, your balance is guaranteed not to go down. There are three main ways the annuity could profit in an up market.

First, they could pay you on the point to point basis. This simply means that if on November 28 of year one the market was at 10,000, and one year later it was at 10,500, you would see a gain of 5% or $500 on your investment.

THE CATCH: This investment form usually comes with a cap on how much you can earn. The caps can change each year and are dependent upon several factors of which one is interest rates and the other is the cost of options in the market.

Over the last 14 years that FIAs have been offered, I would say the average Point to Point Cap in my own experience has been around 5-8% depending on the insurance company and product. In 2001, Caps of annuities my firm represented were as high as 15%. This means you would secure 100% of the market gain up to the cap each year, but in no case could you lose money or your previous gains if the market went negative.

Are you beginning to see the value of this to a retiree?

Second, the annuity might pay you on what is called a monthly average. This means they average the gains and losses of each month in the first contract year (both positive and negative). If the average is positive, that is your gain. If it is negative, again you can't lose money. In 2010, I had many clients using this approach and make 15 - 20%. The client who did the best actually made 43% for one year and can never again lose that gain.

THE CATCH: With this approach, the market could have a large number of negative months and then sky rocket at the end with a gain. The investor here would not make a gain as the "average" was negative.

An example would be that one year the market was up 10% and one of my clients only made 1%. Obviously, they were disappointed. However, the next year the market was up 8% and my client made 10%. Why? Because the market was mostly positive each month that year and only took a dip at the end and therefore the average was higher than the end result.

Thirdly, there is the monthly sum approach. I haven't used this approach in the past 10 years as it is best suited for when you believe we are in a bull market. This approach gives you a capped gain each month based on positive months. However, you could get an uncapped loss for each month the market is negative (keeping in mind you can't lose your money).

An example of a monthly cap might be around 2.5% per month. This is how it might look over a four month period:

Month	Market	Annuity Credit or Debit
January	+2%	+2%
February	+4%	+2.5% capped
March	- 8%	- 8%

If the market gained each month by at least 2.5%, then an investor could make 30% return on their guaranteed investment. However, if the market made 2% each month for 11 months (22% total for first 11 months) and then lost 24% in the last month, the investor's return would be zero (not a negative 2% as you can only gain and never lose in an FIA). That is why I seldom use this approach in a volatile market. When the market has big swings up, you're capped at maybe 2.5% per month. Keep in mind when it drops in large percentages, there is no limit on the negative credit for the year. Remember *you still cannot lose* your money or any previous year's earnings even if the result for the year is a negative 30%! The monthly cap can be a great consideration in *bull market conditions*.

In an FIA, you can change which allocation you want from year to year. You can go from point to point in year one to monthly cap the next or to monthly average the year after that. You are never committed to any choice you or your advisor might make for more than one year. You can also mix and match. You could do 50% in the point to point, 25% in monthly average, and 25% in monthly cap or any combination you desire based on which one or multiples of them would give you the best chance for gain in that year.

For the rest of this chapter, I will be illustrating with the monthly average approach.

Back to our investor who deposited $100,000. Let's say the monthly average of the index that first year went up 10%. Your investment balance would now be $110,000. Your account balance "resets" each year on the anniversary date in most FIAs. That means that once you have earned the gain ($10,000) you can never give it back.

Let's say in year two the index went down by 40%. You would still have $110,000. Not bad, but here is even greater news. Even though you didn't lose any money during the market crash, the insurance company reinvests your $110,000 at the point the index is at on your anniversary (which is down 40%) and *you now start earning for year three from that point.* If the monthly average took the gain for year three up another 10% (even though the index is still down from the 40% loss) then your balance would now be $121,000 EVEN THOUGH THE DOW IS STILL WAY BELOW IT'S LEVEL FROM 2 YEARS EARLIER! You don't have to wait for the market to get back to its previous high! WOW!

THE CATCH: It is important that you understand that FIAs were never designed to compete with a stock or stock mutual fund. Over any period of time an FIA's returns will most likely not perform in tandem with the market and must never be considered as a replacement for an equity portfolio on long-term performance. However, it can possibly make sense for an investor to have *part* of his portfolio in these instruments. In a period like 2000 to 2010, my experience was seeing my clients average a 4-7% rate of return in their FIAs, while the market for buy and hold market investors was much lower if not negative over the same period of time. In a true bull market, it would not be prudent for an investor to expect an FIA to perform anywhere close to that of an actual equity market investment.

Another important point to keep in mind with FIA's is that they all should be considered time deposits. This means that if you draw out your entire balance or more than an annual free withdrawal limit you may be subject to an early withdrawal charge. FIA's can come in terms of anywhere from 5 years or more. I personally don't believe in investing in more than a 10 year FIA.

Most FIA's offer the ability to withdraw 10% of your balance or deposited amount "each year" that you hold the account to give the investor some degree of access to their investment without charge or penalty. If strategized as only a portion of an investor's portfolio this most likely would not in my experience create a hardship on an investor.

Income Riders

Most FIA's also come with an option to add an income rider. Again, with dozens of FIAs being offered, they can all vary. However, let me illustrate a possible income rider with my favorite at the time of this writing.

To illustrate the income rider, divide a piece of paper in two with a line down the middle of it. On the left column write "Market Value" and on the right side "Income Value."

Market Value   Income Value

The income rider comes with a guaranteed growth rate published by the insurance company. For this illustration, let's say it is 8% per year, simple interest. Again assuming someone invested $100,000, the left hand side "Market Value" would grow according to market conditions and which investment option they might choose as illustrated above. However, the "Income Value" would grow by a guaranteed value, of in this case 8%. The chart would then look like this over 4 years:

Monthly Avg. Market ROR	Monthly Avg. Market Value	Income Value
+10%	$110,000	$108,000
-10%	$110,000	$116,000
+ 6%	$116,600	$124,000

If 10 years from now, the market value was only $150,000 (due to poor market conditions) and the income value was $180,000 and you wished to begin taking an income from your FIA, you would be given an income from whichever side was greater. Assuming you took a 5% income that would mean $9,000 per year of income off the $180,000 income value rather than $7,500 off the market value. Of course if the market value was greater, your income would come from that value.

But that's not the end of the story. Many income riders will also give you an increase in income during your retirement years. Your increase each year could be tied to a fixed increase (say 3% each year, regardless of market conditions) or you could have the increase tied to market performance each year. This means instead of a fixed 3% your income might go up 3, 5, 10 or more percent in one year (again based on the market) but in cases where the market was negative in that year you would simply keep the same income as the year before.

Example: Starting income of $9,000 the first year

Year	Monthly Avg Increase	Income
2	+10%	$ 9,900
3	- 5%	$ 9,900
4	+10%	$10,890

Increase could be for your lifetime or could have a fixed number of years they would do this and then freeze the highest payment after a certain period of time. Make sure you check with the company you are considering investing with to get all of the details.

IMPORTANT: Even if you take these incomes and due to the increases, you end up using your entire principal, the insurance company will continue to give you your income until the day you die, even if you have no money left!

IF, however, you have been taking income and still have a balance in the market value side and you are past any early withdrawal charge period, you can decide to cash out and take your accumulation value with you. You never surrender ownership of your principle!

THE CATCH: Though income riders are optional, the insurance company will charge a small fee for this benefit should you select one. Consult the insurance company's investment materials as costs can differ but are usually less than 1%.

It's what I call "Your Own Personal Pension Plan" and guaranteeing your income for life. Do you see a value in this *for part of a retiree's portfolio*? **How about yours?**

CHAPTER 8

Reducing Your Taxes in Retirement to Have More for You and Yours. (Getting the Government Out of Your Pocket)

Is an Ira, Roth IRA, 401K, 403B or 457 plan the best way to go?

Let's first talk about the advantages of these plans and then I will surprise you with all of the problems of these plans and how they can actually come back and hurt not only your retirement, but your loved ones as well.

For many, the saving grace of their retirement will be their company 401k, 403b, 457 or their IRA account. For the last 30 years, this is how most Americans built their retirement portfolios. Why? In my opinion there are three main reasons.

First, for most it was payroll deducted. Once we got use to a certain paycheck (minus our savings), we never missed the money flowing from our paycheck to our retirement plans. You may have even at times forgotten about it until your statement came in the mail showing your new balance.

The second reason company retirement plans were so important for many over the last 30 years was that many employers would "match" or also contribute to your plan. This was free money and anyone who passed it up would have been crazy.

Third, it was tax-deductible from your reportable income each year. You never had to pay tax on money you were paid that went into your retirement account. Accountants and financial planners alike hailed this as a huge opportunity for all Americans and encouraged all to take part.

Now for the bad part;

We were all told to invest now and deduct it as we would most likely be in a smaller tax bracket in retirement so when we withdrew the money, we would pay less tax than while we saved it had we not contributed to a tax-deferred plan.

At the beginning of this book, I discussed many of the current economic events that surround our nation and our financial futures. As you remember, we are now in the second lowest set of tax brackets in the last 93 years and with all of the problems facing our nation economically, we can certainly expect higher taxes and inflation down the road. Therefore, the idea we would pay less in taxes in retirement may not only be incorrect, it could be at a higher rate than what we saved the money at.

If you are still working, I recommend you only contribute to your company retirement plan under one of two conditions:

If your employer is matching your contribution then by all means contribute to get the maximum match. It's free money. However, if there is no company match, I would recommend you instead contribute to a ROTH IRA. As of 2010, the maximum for ROTH contributions for those closing in on retirement was $6,000 per person.

REDUCING YOUR TAXES IN RETIREMENT

If you are married that means $12,000 total for both you and your spouse. For many, this would cover most of what they are putting into a 401K anyway. If you happen to be saving more than the $12,000, then go ahead and put the amount over that in your company plan. At least you will have the lions share in a tax free position.

When clients come in with a fair or sizable amount of tax free money, it is amazing the things that can be done to lower the tax burden on their income in retirement. Allow me to share with you a great example of how funding your tax deductible plan actually can benefit the government more than you.

Tax the Harvest vs. Tax the Seed

Tax the Harvest

Let's say you put away $6,000 per year into a 401k. Let's assume you are in the 25% tax bracket. That would mean you would save approximately $1,500 in taxes that you would have had to pay had you not done the 401k. If you saved the $1,500 per year for 30 years, you saved $45,000 in taxes during your career. It looks like this:

Tax Savings per year: $ 1,500

x 30 years: $45,000

Over a 30 year period of investing let's say you averaged 8% interest on your long-term $6,000 per year. Your investment would have grown to $745,180. Not bad! You saved taxes and have a nice nest egg to boot.

However, now you retire and decide to take an interest income off your retirement plan. Let's assume you could get 6% per year off your $745,180 or an income of $44,711 per year of TAXABLE income. 100% of this income is taxable because you never paid tax on the deposits going into the plan or the growth while in the retirement plan. Assuming your tax rate is still only 25% (most likely it will be higher), your tax on this portion of your retirement income would be. If you are retired for 30 years and pay *$11,178 per year* in taxes that means you will pay the IRS a total amount of *$335,340 in income tax*! Now it looks like this:

Value of retirement plan at time of retirement: $745,180

Income per Year at 6%: $ 44,711

Tax Due on Income at 25%: $ 11,178

Tax You Paid During Retirement: *$335,340* over 30 years

This is called taxing the harvest (the money you rely on for income in retirement).

Let's see now, the IRS let you keep $45,000 in tax savings and in return you gave them $335,340. Wow, what a deal… for the IRS.

Tax the Seed

Let's look at the other option which would mean paying tax on the seed (the money you invested over your working life counting on it growing) rather than on the income you need in retirement.

In our previous example we deposited $6,000 into a tax-deductible retirement plan and by doing so saved $1,500 in taxes each year for a total savings of $45,000. Wouldn't it make more sense to pay the tax on the $6,000 you deposit or $1,500 per year and put the money in a ROTH and then when you withdraw it, you don't pay a penny to the IRS? This would mean paying a total tax over your savings years of $45,000 and then when you draw your retirement income you keep the $335,340 you would have to lose off your retirement income.

If you are currently retired, I will give you some options shortly to recapture as much as possible of the taxes you will be losing. However, if you are still working, you may want to get with your financial advisor and look at some other alternatives to your company retirement plan that can be structured as a ROTH IRA.

The reason you may decide to save through your company plan is if you are concerned about your ability to save without the savings coming out of your paycheck. In other words you're afraid you might not be disciplined enough to receive the money and then save it. If that is the case, I have a suggestion.

Just about any company will allow you to payroll deduct and place money into a savings or checking account at your local bank. To maintain the same idea of saving as you did with your 401k, simply ask your HR department to withhold the desired amount you wish to invest and send it to your bank account. Your personal financial advisor can then set up an auto draft against that account where each month as your bank gets the deposit, they automatically then send it to the investment of your choice. Still payroll deducted, still automatic and still off your paycheck without you seeing it. Now you can set that up as a Roth-IRA which is taxing the seed not the harvest.

You're Retired and Have a Huge Pool of Tax Infested Retirement Money. Now What?

Here are the tax brackets for 2011 as of the writing of this chapter. Washington could change them at ANY time, so make sure you check the rates for the year in which you are reading this book.

Federal Income Tax Brackets for 2013
Based On Taxable Income Ranges

Rate	Single	Married Filing Jointly	Head of Household
10%	$0-8,925	$0-17,850	$0-12,750
15%	$8,925-36,250	$17,850-72,500	$12,750-48,600
25%	$36,250-87,850	$72,500-146,400	$48,600-125,450
28%	$87,850-183,250	$146,400-223,050	$125,450-203,150
33%	$183,250-398,350	$223,050-398,350	$203,150-398,350
35%	$398,350-400,000	$398,350-450,000	$398,350-425,00
39.6%	$400,000 and up	$450,000 and up	$425,000 and up

(Source irs.gov)

Using the Brackets to Convert Tax Infested Money

In a moment, I will share with you how we lower our client's taxable income to the smallest amount possible. However, for your advisor to help you with these tax strategies, it is important that you have some of your assets in either a Roth IRA or in Non-Qualified assets (that is money not in a retirement plan we refer to as NQ) *in addition to any retirement money you hold.*

If you have mostly retirement money, then you need to get some converted to NQ in order for these plans to help you save on taxes. Here is how you can use the brackets to maximize the conversion.

Always be aware of where your taxable income will be each year. This may mean closer communication with your tax advisor. Assume you are a married couple whose taxable income for this year is $75,000. Looking at the brackets just shown, you would not move into the next bracket of 28% until your taxable income is over $137,300. This means that if you decided to convert IRA money to a ROTH-IRA or NQ money this year, you could move up to $62,000 from your IRA assets to a ROTH-IRA or NQ and be sure you will only pay 25% tax on this amount. Whether or not you should do this is based on advice from your tax preparer and your financial professional combined. Although we don't wish to pay any tax, please keep in mind that taxes may be going up significantly in the years ahead. Also, the old capital gains tax rate before it dropped to 15% was at 28%. Back then, this was considered a bargain to only pay a capital gains tax instead of income tax. Please understand that taxes are most likely now on sale! You may want to take advantage of this now.

Converting Tax Infested Money to Non-IRA without the Tax

For years now, the government has given write-offs to people who invested in Gas and Oil Limited Partnerships. There are many to choose from and they come from moderate risk forms of investing to high risk. For a retiree, it may make more sense to stay more toward the conservative side. Whichever way you might choose, the government may give you up to a 100% deduction for investing in these programs. If you were to take IRA money and invest it here, then you would have no tax to pay as the deduction washes against any tax you might owe. Assuming you transferred $50,000 from an IRA to a Gas program that is 100% tax-deductible, it would look like this:

Amount withdrawn from IRA:	$50,000
Tax due at 25%:	$12,500
Deposit into gas program:	$50,000
Tax Savings:	$12,500
Tax due:	$0

This is especially beneficial if you need income as these programs can pay you an income for up to 20 to 30 years and in some cases do so with some additional tax advantages. Consult your financial advisor for ones they might recommend.

Lowering Your Tax Bill Through Wise Income Strategies and Planning

The best way to explain how to do this is not to tell you, but rather show you some examples.

Bill and Mary (names changed)

Bill and Mary came to me for help. Bill had been a barber his entire life and therefore had no pension plan. Here is how their income looked before we met with them.

Social Security	$25,000 (combined)
Income from investments	$18,000
Income from investments (Income not taken or used but earned)	$ 2,000
Total Household Income	$45,000
Tax on Income	$ 2,253
Total take home income	$42,747

How did I arrive at this figure?

As a married couple, if your income (counting 1/2 of your Social Security) equals or exceeds $32,000, then you must claim a portion of your Social Security Income (SSI) and pay tax on it. If your reportable income (counting only 50% of SSI) is below $32,000, then you do not have to claim or pay tax on *any* of your SSI (For single individuals the levels are different, please see your tax advisor for more information on these brackets).

At $32,000, you must claim 50% of your SSI and pay tax on it. For each dollar you make over $32,000, the percentage of your SSI you must claim increases. However, you would never have to claim more than 85% of the SSI you have received regardless of income. Please remember to always consult your tax professional for tax advice. What I share is of general nature and does not reflect state taxes that may be due.

Here is how the taxes came to be for Bill and Mary:

50% of SSI	$12,500
Interest Income	$18,000
Other Interest Earned (Not taken but earned)	$ 2,000

Total Income to determine taxing SSI = $32,500

Before sharing their taxable income, it is important to understand that as a married couple, Bill and Mary get what is called a "Standard Deduction" of $11,400. This can vary depending upon each couple/persons situation, but here is how the IRS shares it on their website, www.irs.gov.

Standard Deduction Amount

The standard deduction amount depends on your filing status, whether you are 65 or older or blind, whether an exemption can be claimed for you by another taxpayer, whether you have a net disaster loss from a federally declared disaster, and whether you paid state or local sales or excise tax (or certain other taxes or fees in a state without a sales tax) in 2010 on the purchase of a new motor vehicle after February 16, 2009, and before 2010. Generally, the standard deduction amounts are adjusted each year for inflation. Use to figure your standard deduction amount.

Bill and Mary had to declare 50% of their SSI income or $12,500. As a result, they must now claim the $32,000 as potentially taxable and here is how I came up with $2,253 of tax:

Reportable Income	$32,500
Minus Standard Deduction	-$11,400
Taxable Income	$21,100
First $16,750 at 10% Bracket =	$1,675
Remaining $3,850 at 15% Bracket =	$578
Total Tax	$ 2,253

That was how it looked when they came in to see us.

The next year they maintained 100% of the same income, but their taxes fell to ZERO!

Here's how we did it.

The $18,000 of income was coming from a NQ tax-deferred annuity and was considered all taxable as the income they were taking represented the interest the annuity was earning. The principal would have been free of tax (because they already paid tax on the deposits), but the interest earned along the way is not. Since the majority of the annuity was created with money that had already been taxed (non IRA), we simply called the annuity company and asked them to annuitize the policy in order to get the same $18,000 and we wanted to know how many years the income would last. It would guarantee the $18,000 for at least 22 years or longer if needed. However, here is the best part. Because the principal in the annuity was non-IRA and had already been taxed, 95% of each payment Bill and Mary received was considered already taxed money and therefore non-taxable as income for the next 22 years. It gets better. Since only 5% of the $18,000 was considered income by the IRS ($900), this dropped their reportable income by $17,100. Therefore, that now means they no longer had to pay tax on *ANY of their SSI.* So here is how the new scenario and taxes looked for Bill and Mary;

50% of SSI	$12,500
Interest Income (reportable)	$ 900
Other Interest Earned (Not taken but earned)	$ 2,000
Total	$15,400

With total reportable income now at = $15,400. Well below the $32,000 magic value. Therefore they did not need to claim or pay tax on the SSI income.

So the "after" picture of their income looked like this;

SSI Reportable Income	$0
Interest Income	$900
Other Interest Earned	$2,000
Minus Standard Deduction	$11,400
Taxable Income (Since below Standard Deduction)	$0

Now an additional income of $2,253 in Bill and Mary's pocket may not seem like a lot to many of you reading this book. However, when your income need is $43,000 and you now get to keep and spend 100% of it and all it took was a phone call, I would guess anyone would accept an additional $2,253 per year to be able to spend. Wouldn't you?

Avoiding Income and Estate Tax for Those You Love with a Charitable Remainder Trusts (CRT's)

It hurts me to think of how much good can be accomplished in the world if retirees would plan ahead. I believe there are two main reasons that most retirees don't plan ahead on what will happen with their estate.

First, some people don't like discussing the subject of their own death and therefore avoid any discussion surrounding it.

Second, it is not the fault of the retiree failing to discuss it, but rather the failure of their professional advisors to do so. This failure on the advisors part can be due to:

a) No concern over it, or

b) Ignorance of this very important subject.

Rather than just talk about the strategy, I feel it is best illustrated.

Jim and Sue Jones

Jim is 71 and Sue is 69. Here is what Jim and Sue's estate looks like:

Home:	$ 300,000
IRA's:	$ 500,000
401-K's	$ 600,000
Non-IRA investments:	$ 250,000
Life Insurance:	$ 100,000
Misc. Assets:	$ 125,000
Total Estate Value:	$1,875,000

In 2011, the estate tax exemption is at $5,000,000. Therefore, no estate tax would be due for this couple. However, they do have over $1,100,000 in retirement accounts that is now subject to income tax at their passing. If their children cashed out the IRA's and 401Ks (which I would say from my personal experience is the case in 85% of clients who have passed) the children would end up owing the federal government about $385,000 as a tax on the retirement accounts.

It would look like this:

Family:	$1,490,000
IRS:	$ 385,000
Charity:	$ 0
Total:	$1,875,000

If Jim and Sue had no charitable intent, they then could use part of the required minimum distribution (RMD) they now pay each year on Jim (and soon on Sue) to buy a $385,000 life insurance policy to cover the taxes and thus leave their children 100% of the value of their estate.

It would look like this:

Family (incl. insurance):	$1,875,000
IRS	$385,000
Charity:	$ 0
Total:	$2,260,000

If Jim and Sue had a charitable intent (American Cancer Society, Church, Missions, Homeless Shelter, etc.), they could use their RMD to once again buy a bit more insurance and *gift their retirement assets to charity*. This gift to charity does not occur until the death of the second spouse. Therefore, they maintain all control of the assets while they are alive. By giving their retirement money to charity at the passing of the second spouse, it is no longer in their estate and thereby no longer taxable to either them or the charity as the charity is of course a non-taxable entity. Now it would look like this:

Family: (incl. insurance of $1.1 mil)	$1,875,000
IRS:	$ 0
Charity:	$1,100,000
Total:	$2,975,000

This is assuming they don't need the RMD to live on and are forced to take them even though they don't need the income. While it is a larger life premium, it protects the family with 100% of the estate they intended to leave them while at the same time providing a legacy in their name to charities that mean something to them.

Bob and Susan Davis

Bob is 65 and Susan is 60. Bob and Susan have no RMD requirements yet. However, earlier we spoke of taxes being on sale at this time. Therefore, they may be ahead by taking out some IRA withdrawals at this time and using them to buy insurance. Here is their current estate:

Home:	$1,100,000
IRA's:	$800,000
401-K's:	$1,150,000
Non-IRA investments:	$475,000
Life Insurance:	$1,000,000
Business Interest:	$2,500,000
Misc. Assets:	$250,000
Total Estate Value:	$7,275,000

Bob and Susan have an estate tax problem as well as an income tax problem at their death.

Estate Tax at 55% (on amount over 5 mil) =	$1,251,250
Income tax on retirement accounts: =	$ 682,500
Total Tax:	$1,933,750

So the inheritance looks like this:

Family:	$5,341,250
IRS:	$1,933,750
Charity:	$ 0
Total:	$7,275,000

Here is the strategy:

If they convert the million dollars of life insurance they already own to an Irrevocable Life Insurance Trust (ILIT), this then removes it from the estate tax calculation and they immediately save $550,000 of tax. This would make sense as they have a larger estate and Susan most likely won't need the insurance money to support her. If they gift their retirement money to charity (remember, this is only done at the death of the second spouse so they never give up control of the money until they are both gone), and use their RMD to replace the retirement money with insurance (again in an ILIT) then the end result looks like this:

Family:	$7,275,000
IRS:	$ 0
Charity:	$1,950,000
Total:	$9,225,000

Let me emphasize that strategies such as this do work. It is important when considering these ideas that you consult both your tax advisor, proper legal counsel, and your financial advisor before making a decision if this is right for you.

I hope this chapter has encouraged you to think about how a little bit of planning can actually protect your estate for your family as well as create a legacy to causes that may be important to you. God bless you as you think this through.

CHAPTER 9

How to Beat the Coming Inflation

In the first Chapter I discussed briefly the problem we face with coming inflation. Allow me to offer just a brief review and then follow up with how you can profit from this phenomenon that I believe is coming fast.

The last time anyone has seen any degree of inflation worth talking about was back in 1980-81 when inflation hit 21.5%. That was 30 years ago! Based on the rule of 72 (when you divide the rate of return into the number 72) you get 3.35 which is how many years it took for the cost of living to double.

Take a minute and think about that. If you were in retirement during that time, the cost of a loaf of bread or a gallon of gas or a pound of hamburger was doubling in cost every 3.35 years at that rate. How do you handle that on a retiree's income? How could your investment portfolio keep pace with the increasing costs to provide you the necessary interest income without running into your principal? In the 36 years before 1981, inflation would hit us, on average, about three times within each 18 year period or once every 6 years.

If inflation happened three times over each 18 year period from 1944 to 1981, what happened over the last 31 years that we haven't seen any significant inflation? One possible answer is that the Federal Reserve (Fed) has had inflation under control by controlling the rate of interest that banks pay to borrow money. This then passes down to the consumer. Each time consumers start to spend too much money thereby adding to inflation, and the Fed would raise interest rates ever so slightly to discourage more borrowing by consumers and thereby lessen demand which can help toward lowering the inflation rate. If consumers weren't consuming enough, then the Fed might lower interest rates to encourage borrowing and stimulate the economy. So where does that leave us today?

Today we have a unique problem. The economy has been falling for several years now and continues to do so with truly no relief in sight. The problem is that the Fed has been lowering interest rates for years now and it still has not stimulated the economy. President Obama resorted to stimulus packages using trillions of tax payer money in an effort to stimulate the economy. While it had some effect, it was a small and not a lasting effect resulting in not much more than a bandage on the economy. If a stimulus by the government hasn't worked and rates can't be lowered as we are at the lowest interest rate period in modern history, what's left?

What's left, in my opinion, is that one of the worst inflation times of modern history will return for two reasons. First, as stated earlier the Fed has printed almost three trillion dollars of new U.S. currency and flooded the markets with them. As you now know, this is extremely inflationary. Second, while I believe inflation will start small as the economy does eventually revive and demand picks up, the problem will grow to potentially never before seen inflation levels.

What Can You do to Protect Your Income From the Demands of Inflation?

There are two paths I can recommend.

First I would consider investing in gold

I never seem to stop hearing from people that gold is a bad buy because it is in a bubble. I have to almost chuckle each time I hear this. One financial radio personality is famous for saying, "Don't buy gold. It's in a bubble." He has been saying this for as long as I can remember. Yet, gold just continues to climb in value.

Please, please, please remember this: everything is at some time or another in a bubble! I remember the year I started working in the financial arena was 1981. Everyone was talking the next year (when the Dow first hit 1,000) how the Dow was in a bubble and to get out NOW! Of course you know the rest of the story. The Dow was in a bubble all right and the bubble lasted until the Dow hit 14,000.

Of course gold is in a bubble. That's not the question. The real question is when might the bubble burst?

When investing in anything, always start with the fundamental question which is: What is causing the value of this item or commodity (in this case gold) to go up in value and are the fundamental causes still in place to cause it to continue to go up? If the answer is yes, then we should not worry about the current value as much as we should think about the potential future value.

What's happening that could cause the price of gold to continue to rise? Let me share a few thoughts as to why I *believe* this is the case. First, it seems to me that China is now raising up a middle class economically more so than they have had before due to more companies opening plants there and creating more jobs among other reasons. In the past in China it seemed you were thought of as either rich or poor. The middle class was a weak, if not missing, element. Now, with many American manufacturers opening in China, many of their people, once in the poor column, suddenly now have gainful employment. What are these new workers in China doing with their money? While I cannot say for sure I believe they are saving and investing it in gold! Why? Because I believe they don't trust their government or its currency and they do not know if their new found prosperity will last.

What about India? I believe the same thing is transpiring there. What about Russia? I believe the same is happening in these countries as well!

If you were living in Greece right now, would you put your money in Greek banks? Would you put it in Greek government bonds? I don't think so.

The currency of Europe, the Euro, is in dire straits. Do you think European citizens are betting and investing in the Euro?

What about the good old USA? Do you think many are worried about the future of our currency? Do you think many are worried about the possibility that we could follow the ways of Greece, Italy, Ireland, or Portugal? Can we at least admit that faith in most countries and their government's currency, or even their government, is not at an all-time high? Where do people go when they have lost faith? They go to gold. The fundamentals are there and I believe will continue to be for quite some time until we work through all of the economic problems we face worldwide.

How should you buy gold?

While I will leave it to each individual to identify how they prefer to invest in the golden metal, I do have some options for you.

You can buy actual gold bullion. This can be done in bricks of gold or in the form of gold coins minted by various governments.

A gold brick isn't the same size as a regular brick like you would build a house out of. It is a bit larger (2 cubic inches larger). I will assume you are thinking about gold bar (like that stored at Fort Knox) and the standard for international transactions. A gold bar weighs 400 Troy ounces... that is 27.4 pounds. With a density of 0.698 pounds per cubic inch and the bar having a volume of about 39 cubic inches (a regular brick is 6″ x 3″ x 2″ and has 36 cubic inches of volume) the value varies daily and is reported on the gold market per Troy ounce. As of this writing, gold was at about $1,650 per ounce. At that price you would take 400 x $1,650 = $1,302,400 for each brick in U.S. Dollars. Needless to say for most of us that would be a bit out of our league.

For this reason, most people who wish to own and hold gold do so by buying gold coins. U.S. coins are offered in 1/10 oz., 1/4 oz., 1/2 oz., and 1 oz. denominations. These coins are guaranteed by the U.S. government to contain the stated amount of actual gold weight in troy ounces. This makes owning gold much more convenient and easy to store.

Another way to own gold is to buy an "Exchange Traded Fund" or ETF. When buying an ETF, you are buying shares of ownership in the bullion itself, but in the form of shares not the actual metal. The advantage of this is much cheaper costs to own the metal, ease of storage, and immediacy of both buying and selling your shares on the open market.

If you buy gold and hold it in your possession, the commissions and fees can be anywhere from 3% to 8%. This is money not going into the value of gold, but rather pure up front and backend costs to both buy it and sell it. In addition there are shipping costs.

If you buy the gold in the form of an ETF fund, you would only be paying a brokerage commission. If done through an online trading site, this can be as low as $7 to $10 regardless of the amount of shares you might buy.

Second, I would consider investing in High Grade Rare Coins You most likely have never heard of High Grade Rare Coins (HGRC) before. Neither had I until 1997. First let's talk about what a HGRC is. Collectable coins come in different grades from MS-40 to MS-70 or PF-40 to PF-70. HGRCs are only those coins at a rating of 65 or higher. While all coins can benefit from rising interest rates and inflation, the very best opportunities are in those rated as 65 or higher.

To get an idea of just what coins can do, we can look back at the last time we had significant inflation in the early 80's. During that time (over a period of approximately 2 years), some HGRC's increased in value by over 1,000%. That means if you had $10,000 in HGRC's, it could have grown to more than $100,000. $20,000 could have possibly grown to $200,000 depending on the coin or coins you owned!

While I'm sure you don't need me to tell you how valuable that could be to you the next time rates rise and inflation comes back, allow me to share some strategies in how coins can be used to help you not run out of income.

Let's say you have an investment portfolio of $1,000,000. Assuming you had $500,000 of it in red money, and the market loses 40% and interest rates begin to rise, and you thereby lose $200,000 (40% of the $500,000), imagine if you had a coin(s) that were worth $20,000. They would now be potentially worth over $200,000, which in a sense could have replaced your lost red money. While past performance may not be indicative of future performance it could in any form of possible return be a bonus to help you recoup your possible losses in other investments.

If you are balancing your portfolio properly as I discussed in earlier chapters, HGRC's can add to your diversification and improve the balance you have while protecting your buying power.

It is important to note that as with any investment or commodity that HGRC's can also lose value. Should interest rates fall in the future rather than go up in value, it would only be logical that the value of your coins could fall as well. So, the big question is; "Which way do you see rates going over the coming years?

I get many questions from clients on HGRC's. Allow me to answer the most popular ones at this time.

What is the lowest price I might expect to pay for a HGRC?

Usually to get a 65 rated coin would start around $3,000.

Do I hold the coin after I buy it?

Yes. I would recommend invest the $35 or so needed to get a safety deposit box. Never keep the coin in your home in case of a fire.

How would I sell my coin? Who would buy a coin for $100,000 that I paid $10,000 for?

There are coin auctions around the country each month that work very similar to the stock market. At the time you wish to sell you would send or deliver your coin to your coin dealer who would then take it to auction. You never have to find a buyer. The more inflation that takes place, the higher the demand for HGRCs and the more you can sell it for.

How much can I lose on my coin?

Coins go up and down in value based mostly on the rise and fall of interest rates. According to a Yahoo Finance report in 2012, 13 week Treasury bonds are at their lowest rate since 1960. Ask any person you know regardless of age "When was the last time you saw rates this low?" The answer would most likely have to be NEVER. Though there could be small number of reasons for a coin losing its value, one of the primary causes would be falling interest rates. My question is how low can rates go? Now the real question; Do you believe rates are more likely to go up or down over the next 5 years? Most everyone I ask seems to say UP! This then could bode well for someone to consider owning HGRCs.

Is there a commission to buy coins?

Yes. Coin dealers vary in their charges and fees. A reasonable fee would be around 15 -20%. While this may sound high, remember a coin costing you $10,000 (meaning immediate value might be $8,000) if it goes up by 400% could now be worth $32,000. It's still a 300% increase. By the way, when you sell your coin, the fees usually drop as most coin dealers adjust their selling fees relative to the size of the sale.

Most important, it is imperative you find a coin dealer or financial advisor you trust to lead you to the right coins in order to make sure you don't get taken advantage of. HGRCs are something most people know little about and that's when you can be taken advantage of. Make sure you find advisors and dealers you can trust.

The coin professional's viewpoint

I have been working with one expert in the HGRC industry over the past 15 years to help my clients find the very best in HGRC's. His name is Anthony Scirpo of Farmington Valley Rare Coins in New Hartford, CT. Tony has 48 years of experience and is the only one I personally trust in this specialized area of investing. I asked Tony if he would mind sharing some in his own words on the subject and opportunities with HGRC's. The following is what Tony wanted to share with you.

The Rare Coin Advantage

More than likely you never heard of High Grade Rare Coins, [HGRC], and just as likely, you never knew that they were and are the world's number one ranked asset, moreover, they can actually become "mainstream assets," and much more needed and desirable during certain economic conditions, which we shall visit later.

What Are High Grade Rare Coins?

Thirty or so years ago, if you ventured into the then relatively small circle of investment quality rare coins, you were taking quite a gamble. The "gamble" was ascertaining the numismatic grade of the coin, (see the following Technical Notation). As with diamonds, but on an even more discerning, sophisticated basis, it is the grade thereof that controls and/or establishes market price. Again, as with diamonds, the proven combination of rarity and quality dictate what is and what is not a truly rare coin.

TECHNICAL NOTATION: The rare coin market evaluates mint state, {or uncirculated coins}, and proof issues, utilizing an Eleven Point Grading System. It has a low of Mint State/Proof-60, [MS-60/ PF-60], to a high of MS/PF-70, the latter representing the perfect coin, (a grade that no rare coin made prior to 1965 has ever received or will receive). The grade "65" is indicative of a gem uncirculated specimen, be it a proof or a mint state, (business strike), example. All coins in grade PF-67 or higher, (or MS-67 or higher), are classified as "wonder coins," and that achievement and the precious few that attain it, are prohibitively rare, (beyond scarce). END OF TECHNICAL NOTATION.

While no market or investment can ever be guaranteed or subject to warranty, including rare coins and the rare coin market, we can call upon a unique facet of that market to give us a better to best chance of making fruitful gains on our investment in rare coins. The steps in the solution are two-fold... first and foremost, it is absolutely essential to retain an experienced rare coin professional. This has to be someone who is very familiar with the certified rare coin market and with strong ties and a complete understanding of the certification process and the empirical data that has grown out of it; second, and just as important, always buy top quality, high grade rare coins, that are certified, by the Numismatic Guaranty Corporation of America (NGC), or The Professional Coin Grading Service (PCGS). We prefer NGC owing to their totally objective operating procedures and their pro-consumer products, services and practices.

High Grade Rare Coins have retained their historical number one ranked status for generations, at least extending back to 1965. The former Salomon Brothers, a large New York City brokerage, published a much-awaited, annual survey for many years, and top quality rare coins were always first on the survey listing. In more recent times, (2007-2010), the Penn State Survey has taken center stage as the dominating, most objective evaluation of several assets... gold bullion, the stock market, Three-Month T-Bills, Ten-Year Treasury Bonds, and three categories of rare coins. The Penn State Survey covered over 30 years commencing in 1979. The asset that gained the most were rare coins in MS-65 grade, well ahead of gold, government bills and bonds, and stocks. The survey also revealed still one more heart-pounding advantage of rare coins... they had the highest correlation to inflation or, put in other words, top quality, high grade rare coins, performed the best during inflationary times... and they still do.

Inflation and Proper Asset Allocation

Inflation is an insidious phenomenon and we believe it to be as misunderstood, [if understood at all], of its effects on our investments, savings, and daily living. To begin with, many people think that "inflation" is tantamount to rising costs of goods and services. Technically, this is wrong. Inflation is actually the printing of currency. The result of "inflation" or monetary inflation is an unruly increase in the monetary supply and that ultimately results in "price inflation" which we are more familiar with and what most of us call "inflation."

I believe that during times of minor inflation, an allocation of one's investment dollars belongs in rare coins. This will give your portfolio some balance and protect against paper market volatility and downward spikes in other investment assets. During anticipated periods of serious price inflation, the allocation should be increased... just as seriously as the threat of significant price inflation and/or hyperinflation may dictate. In short, if you see an economic trainwreck coming and it's in the form of significant price inflation, the asset with the highest correlation thereto happens to be High Grade Rare Coins, a.k.a. top quality, certified American rare coins. As with all battles to be waged, we have to know the enemy, [inflation/ price inflation], and determine which weapons will protect us... and then we have to act prudently and get enough of whatever to do the job. Anything less and our financial plan, not to mention financial future, will be placed at greater risk. History has more than proven this and to essentially quote Spanish-born, American philosopher Jorge Augustin Santayana, "He who ignores the mistakes of history is doomed to repeat history's mistakes." This applies to every facet of our lives and is just as applicable, if not even more so, in finance and economics

Rare Coin Performance During the Last Serious Price Inflationary Spiral

From 1978/79 to 1982/83, a time of very high monetary and price inflation, home mortgage interest rates ran anywhere from 19%-21%+ and even as late as 1986, [and with perfect credit and a 50%+ down payment], the best home mortgage interest rate was 10 1/2%. To give you an idea of high grade rare coin performance during that time frame, nearly all meaningful issues went up over 300%, and 500% was common-place, but the really good rare coin material, the top quality certified, high grade specimens that we advocate, broke through 1000% and some went to a reported 1,165% or 11.65 times the money originally invested. Not that this result was unequaled by any other market, tangible or intangible, but it wasn't a "flash in the pan."

The present inflation forecast is much worse than the one experienced in the late 70s and early 80s; in fact, it is quite possible that we could endure hyperinflation. The borrowed cost of the VietNam War figured predominantly in the last inflationary spiral and the cost of the Mid-East Wars is in the trillions of dollars this time around. In addition, federal budget deficits are currently over $1.2 trillion or more and projected at that level out as far as 2019. The United States already has a record public debt of $15+ trillion and to service this debt, [interest alone], costs us just over $500 billion...and there's no end in sight. Worse still, there are the so-called "un-funded" governmental obligations such as Social Security, Medicare, federal pensions, and trade deficits that are as staggering as they are record-breaking. All-in-all, the overall liability picture is why the U.S. Fed is pumping more and more money into what is currently a depressed economy. The bottom line: government's answer to spiraling, out-of-control debt is to "monetize" that debt. In other words, crank up the government printing press and print more dollars, over half of which are held outside of the United States and waning quickly. The U.S. dollar is the world's currency, [of last resort], a phenomenon that arose out of the Bretton Woods, [New Hampshire], Agreement of what was then the immediate, post WW-II, G-7 nations. The dollar is losing that status and therefore the weeks and months that the U.S. Fed can "order up" our present fiat currency are at risk. Any abandonment of the U.S. Dollar, including a partial one, will see most of the currency held outside of the U.S. sent back. This alone could easily cause horrendous price inflation, i.e., the vast amount of money pursuing all too few goods and services

One of the prime purposes of the rare coin asset is to guard against inflation and, quite frankly, to help you profit during times of inflation. Inflation, in any of its faces, is disaster to almost all stocks and paper market issues and it won't take much to turn this country's financial/economic balance on its ear. In fact, just a repeat of the 70s and 80s style of inflation will do it. Unfortunately, the forecasts are calling for much more inflation and possibly continuing for a long period of time. It will be a time in which fortunes are lost and for a few, fortunes will be made...history so dictates. The best asset that I know of, and to again repeat, the very best asset to have in tow during an inflationary spiral, is high grade rare coins.

Closing Remarks

As we circumferentially indicated earlier, the prime directives of success in the rare coin market is the selection of a proper rare coin professional and, of course, the acquisition of the best coins that one can afford. Quite frankly, if coins in the price range of $3000, at a minimum, are not affordable for you, it would be best not to buy rare coins. Focus on debt reduction, cash accumulation, and perhaps buy gold and silver bullion, Bullion anything, however, will not put you "ahead" of inflation... it will only, (hopefully), keep you "even" with it.

Thanks, Tony, for your contribution and education on High Grade Rare Coins and Inflation.

(www.tradingeconomics.com/united-states/inflation-cpi)

(www.makethelist.net/ten-famous-coin-collectors/)

CHAPTER 10

My Success in the End

In this final chapter, I will share with you the greatest secret of my success. However, I must begin this chapter with a warning label. I have no intention of holding anything back. It is my story. Therefore, it may not be what you would expect. But to write it with anything less than the truth or what it is or was would be an injustice.

Depending on your background, your faith and your upbringing, you may find some of this offensive or uncomfortable. I apologize in advance if this is the case. However, it's my story. If you would be easily offended, then please stop now and read no further. If you stop reading at this time thank you for allowing me the privilege of sharing and having a small part in your life. I trust the information provided has helped and will continue to help you find financial freedom.

Now, for those of you still with me, allow me to share something greater than financial freedom. In order to convey the secret to my success, I need to go back in time a bit.

When I was younger, I was blessed with parents who constantly encouraged me and told me how I could do most anything and someday I would be a great success. I eventually began to believe it and anytime something good happened in my life, I would say, "Gee, look at that; my folks must be right! Maybe I am going to be successful!" It wasn't that I didn't make a ton of mistakes and do things wrong; I just focused and hung on to those things I did right.

The successes built on themselves, especially in the early years. Out of four children born to Marvin and Norah Whipple, I was the only one who finished college. It's not because I was better or smarter than my brothers and sisters, it was because I "had" to finish college. Let me explain. I had a dream in my heart that was planted when I was 16 years old. I decided that I wanted to be a disc jockey on the radio. However, then it went further. I also decided to own and run 14 radio stations across the United States. Why 14? At the time, it was the maximum amount you could own by law. I had intended these radio stations to be such that they would have a positive impact on the lives of young people across America. An impact that would help kids and young adults learn and believe that they could find success and happiness in life.

While in college, I worked at the college radio station, and the miracles began to happen. I did some on air time and creative work with my professor, Dr. Tom Nash at Biola University. He quickly became one of my hero's in life. Dr. Nash asked me if I would help, by trying to sell some advertising time around the community to help raise money and support the station. Now, the station only reached the students on campus. So, I decided at first to stick with the local retailers interested in reaching the student body.

One day, I decided to call an advertising agency in Los Angeles. Here's this tiny little school of 4,500 students and I'm calling an ad agency with marble counters on the top floor of a Los Angeles skyscraper. To my amazement, I got the appointment, and even more surprisingly, got the account. My sales success was so great, that I continued to build the revenues for our little station, beyond anyone's expectations. In my senior year, I decided to approach a "real" radio station off campus about selling for them part-time. I got the job at KYMS in Santa Ana and sold so many ads, that I was equaling the sales of the full timers on a part time basis. After graduation, I married my sweetheart, Connie Johnson, back in Michigan and we moved to California where I worked full time in radio sales. Immediately, I began meeting with a college buddy named Wally Hollis. He and I began putting together a proposal to buy and own our first station at the ripe ages of 23 and 22. We identified a station in Detroit, Michigan (I thought we'd start with a tiny market) that I had spoken to the owner and was given the impression we could buy for $3.5 million. In 1980, that was a bunch of money! We spent over 6 months preparing the presentation and plan.

There was only one problem, where would two college grads, come up with $3.5 million? According to a bank that showed any interest at all, we would have to come up with one million dollars of down payment, in order to have a chance of financing the rest. While in college, I met a guy who had an uncle in Michigan who ran a rather large drapery business. I called his Uncle and asked if we could meet, explaining the idea and a potential ownership position in the new station. He said he would listen so Wally, my wife, Connie, and I flew to Detroit to stay with her parents and make our pitch.

As we walked into the meeting, the drapery owner and his right hand man walked into the room and were immediately set back by our apparent youth. I guess they were expecting more. However, by the end of the meeting they committed $100,000 to the two young college grads! Not knowing where else to go, we asked them if they knew any other business owners that may be willing to listen to the same opportunity. They gave us the names of two brothers and a sister who owned auto parts stores in the Metro area. Again, we met with surprise at our age, but by the time we were done, they committed $300,000 to the plan. By the end of the two weeks, we had raised $500,000 of the $1,000,000 needed. However, we ran out of time and needed to get back to our jobs in L.A. We decided to come back and find the other $500,000 in two weeks.

During the two weeks in L.A., I received notice that the station we had planned to purchase was sold to Doubleday Broadcasting for 8.3 million dollars! We lost our bid.

I remained at KYMS for a while and almost immediately became sales manager. Times were good. Connie was working at Ford Aerospace in Newport Beach, and we both enjoyed a beautiful new home, more income than we could have dreamed of, a 280-Z as a company car at the radio station, and did I say more money than we could have dreamed of? We were making about $75,000 per year combined. In 1979, that was a lot of money However, the dream of developing stations having a positive impact on young people was still lingering in my heart.

I felt it was important, that if I was going to run stations of my own, I better get some experience as a station manager, rather than only a sales manager. I was reading Broadcasting Magazine, and noticed an ad for a General Manager (GM) position at a station in the St. Louis, MO market. I was 26 years old. I didn't know it, but that was considered way too young to have any hope of getting a position like that, especially in a top 20 market at the time. Guys my age would be lucky to get a GM job in Podunk, USA.

Still, I applied for the job. By this time, I was getting used to the shocked looks I would receive when people first met me and realized my age. I got the same look on this interview. Skipping the details, I got the job! To my knowledge, I was the youngest GM in a top 20 market anywhere in the country.

Sounds like life was just too good to be true. Things were going great. I was moving up the ladder, and in my eyes, there was no stopping me.

The Bad Times Begin!

The station I took the GM job at was not one of the strongest stations in St. Louis… OK, it was pathetic! It was ranked 42 out of 42 in the ST. Louis ARB ratings. But that didn't scare me. I had just come from one of the top stations in Orange County, California. I was so confident in my abilities by this point, that I know this is where God decided it was time to allow me to learn that ultimately, it wasn't all up to me and I couldn't do it all by myself. It also is where my lessons in financial freedom began to build.

As Connie and I began to look for our new home in St. Louis, we settled on one across the Mississippi river in Belleville, Illinois. It was a gorgeous house that frankly, we didn't need but fell in love with. It was more than we could afford at the time. However, I had been promised bonuses on any business generated above the current cash flow of the station and just knew I would have the station "rockin' and rollin'" in no time at all. So, I bought the house. Though the station immediately started growing in listeners, it wasn't growing as quickly as I had hoped. Income was still not up to par and Connie had just given birth to our daughter, Kelly. As parents, we felt strongly about the importance of Connie being a full-time mom and, therefore, went from the two big incomes in California to just the one small one in St. Louis, with a huge mortgage on our new home. The home that I felt would be the envy of our friends became our most humiliating and humbling embarrassment. We purchased the home in 1981 and if you're old enough, you'll remember the double-digit inflation and interest rates back at that time. Our home mortgage was at a very high interest rate and resulted in outrageous payments each month. As a result, we lived in a "palace" with virtually no furniture since we couldn't afford to buy any. We lived in a fish bowl, as we also couldn't afford drapes. One day, while eating dinner, we both jumped, as a total stranger walked up on the deck (came with the house) out the back sliding doors and pushed his face up against the glass. With cupped hands around his eyes, he was staring into our kitchen trying to get a glimpse of the inside of this empty house that surely must be for sale. Both parties were embarrassed.

I began to come home from work each day and find Connie sitting on the love seat (the only piece of furniture we had outside of the kitchen and bedroom), crying because that day, she had received 5 phone calls from creditors demanding payments on the credit cards.

I knew something had to be done!

Pressures were beginning to grow. The station was not perform-
ing as well as I had planned and the owners were beginning to
put the squeeze on me to put more and more "garbage" on the air,
just to make more money. It was about that time, that I had an old
friend come by and offer to sell me some life insurance. Not knowing I didn't have a dime to put toward it, he made his best pitch.
This was "cool" life insurance, called Universal Life. It was brand
new at the time, and you actually could make money and build
your financial future by owning it. I asked my friend how much
he made by selling it and then asked if they were hiring part time
sales people. I got the job part time and immediately found some
small success. We began paying off some bills and eventually; I
was made an offer to work full-time in life insurance sales. I had
to do something to stop the financial pain and free my wife from
the creditors. I was getting the "squeeze" from the owners at the
station and decided it was time to move on and go where I felt I
could support the family.

I'll never forget the day I came home from the radio station with
the decision to enter the life insurance business full-time. I don't
ever recall crying so hard and shedding so many tears. The dream,
for now, had died!

Too much more of my story, I'm afraid, would cause great pain
for you to read…in more ways than one. I quickly went from life
insurance sales to financial planning and in 1986, began my own
financial planning firm C. Curtis & Associates. Each step along
the way has been filled with failures, yet many successes as well.

The point to all of this is that I found, in my own strength, I am
very limited. No matter how good I think I am…or how bad, there
had to be more to life than just money and climbing the corporate
ladder. I always felt that the more money I made the greater of a
success I would become. The bigger my house, the fancier the car,

the grander the trips and vacations, the more of a success I would be. But what happens when I die? Do I take it with me? Is life about how much money I can accumulate? Or, is there more?

I, by no means, have ever been financially rich as most would see it. Compared to modern day athletes and movie stars and large corporate executives, I was a little guy. Oh, but how I wanted to swim with the big fish. I wanted to swim with them so bad, I was willing to ruin my life, and the lives of the ones I loved the most, trying to get it.

As a financial planner, I have sat with people who were multi-millionaires to those totally broke, and realized they could be equally unhappy, regardless of their level of income or position. As a matter of fact, in many cases, I found the wealthy ones tended to be unhappier than the ones without any money. I've known friends who were well off financially and yet still miserable. If money buys happiness, why are so many wealthy people ruining their lives with it? You see, the truly rich people will all tell you money is only important to a certain point. Once you have enough of it, it just doesn't matter anymore. It's not important. That's why rich people can be miserable. Because, their whole life, they've lived by the misconception that money buys happiness. When they finally get the money and they still aren't happy, they begin trying all sorts of weird stuff to find happiness. It's why so many famous and rich people ultimately sink their own ship. If money and fame aren't the answer to happiness, what is?

First, don't get me wrong: we should always strive to be financially free. Financial freedom can mean no bondage to creditors. The point is we don't have to be financially rich to be financially free. However, there's one more thing to add.

Along my journey, I was also developing a closer relationship, with God. Note I didn't say religion, rather a relationship. This relationship, in itself, is a lifelong journey that never ends. With each year of my life, the relationship tends to grow stronger and deeper. Each time I begin to think I'm wise, I quickly realize there is much more to learn. I'm sure this will continue until the day I die.

Have you ever noticed that at each stage of life you sometimes think how ignorant you were at younger ages? At 21, I thought I was so mature. I would look back at the high school students (who thought they knew it all) and think of how immature they were. At 35, I couldn't believe how naive I was at 21. I think you get my point. The same seems to be true of my relationship with God. At each stage of my life, I would have times that I thought I had it all together. I felt in communion with God, family relationships were strong, and financially things were good. It would always seem about then, that I would learn another lesson in life.

Connie and I have two of the most beautiful children you can imagine. Inside and out, our children constantly bring us happiness as parents. They've made their mistakes and caused us grief at times, as any teenager or child would. But overall, we couldn't imagine two children providing us with greater joy. Are our children this way because we were such awesome parents? No way! We did our best. However, the results are truly a blessing of God and He gets all the credit.

Whenever our toughest times and lessons in life would surface, we would find ourselves looking for answers in the Bible. The closer our relationship with God would be, the more peace, joy, and happiness we would find. Then, things may get going really good again, and suddenly, God was in the back seat. It was as if I was saying, "Okay, God, thanks for getting me this far, I can take it from here!" Then after a time of doing it my way, I would once again mess it all up and it was time to seek God again.

I have found God to be real and living and very much involved in my life. He is anxious to be part of your life regardless of your past. It's through this relationship that Connie and I have found true happiness. However, it comes from a source we seldom think of, our Creator.

Financial freedom (no debt and a content lifestyle) can add to our family's happiness, being financially rich doesn't. In Philippians 4:12 & 13 of the Bible, Paul says; "I know what it is to be in need and I know what it is to have plenty. I have learned the secret of being *content in any and every situation*, whether well fed or hungry, whether living in plenty or in want. I can do all things through Him who gives me strength." It is in this relationship with God that happiness is found. You can't take all your wealth with you when you die. I heard it said once that I've never seen a Brinks truck following a hearse. I've also heard it said that money just shifts from one person to the next. As we journey through life, we accumulate money. Then when we die, the money is dispersed to others and the cycle starts all over again. However, no one ever really "owns" it.

Are you trying to find happiness through obtaining more money? Read the magazines! Read about the lives of so many who do have the money. Are they truly the happiest people? Or, are those who have a relationship with family, those financially free, and those who have a relationship with their Creator the ones who are truly rich and successful in life?

In Mark 8:36 it says, *"What good is it for a man to gain the whole world, yet forfeit his soul?"* Are you spending all of your time trying to get more money? Take a look around you. You'll find more treasure than you could ever imagine, right within your own household, your own family, and a relationship with God.

John 3:16 say's "For God loved the world so much that He gave is one and only Son, so that everyone who believes in Him will not perish but have eternal life" (NLT). I can't earn my relationship with Him, it is only found in a FREE "gift" of belief in His Son.

I have found my relationship with God comforts me in times of stress, worry, anxiety, and fear. If you would like to know more about this relationship, I would like to recommend a book: *The Prodigal God* by Tim Keller

I know the ideas presented in this book you just read can provide you the tools to finding financial freedom. Now, it's up to you. Will you use them? While finding your financial freedom may take time, it will happen if you're patient. The Living Bible says, "But these things I plan won't happen right away. Slowly, steadily, surely, the time approaches when the vision will be fulfilled. If it seems slow, do not despair, for these things will surely come to pass. Just be patient! They will not be overdue by a single day." Habakkuk 2:3

Now, allow me to leave you with this prayer found in Colossians 1:11 & 12.

"We pray that you will be filled with his mighty, glorious strength so that you can keep going, no matter what happens—always full of the joy of the Lord, and always thankful to the Father, who has made us fit to share all the wonderful things that belong to those who live in the kingdom of light."

May God richly bless you and yours. May you find financial freedom and the true riches you seek in life.